MW00874728

Columbia River near Astoria

Building Oregon's Coast Highway 1936-1966:

Straightening Curves and Uncorking Bottlenecks

By Joe R. Blakely

Author of
Lifting Oregon Out Of The Mud: Building the Oregon Coast Highway and
OSWALD WEST - Governor of Oregon 1911-1915

Copyright © 2014
by Joe Blakely

All rights reserved. No part of the material protected
by this copyright notice may be reproduced or
utilized in any form or by any means, electronic or
mechanical, including photocopying,
recording or by any informational
storage and retrieval system
without written permission from the copyright owner.

First Edition, 2014

Cover photos:

Front: Neahkahnie Overlook
Back: Astoria Ferry Terminal

Published by
Groundwaters Publishing, LLC

P.O. Box 50, Lorane, Oregon 97451
http://www.groundwaterspublishing.com

ISBN-13: 978-1500679385
ISBN-10: 1500679380

I wish to dedicate this book to
my good friend, William Sullivan,
mentor and editor extraordinaire.

Acknowledgments

Oregon's Coast Highway has been my passion ever since my first book *Lifting Oregon Out Of The Mud*.

My new book, *Building the Oregon Coast Highway 1936-1966* was put together with a community of help.

First off, William Sullivan did most of the editing. With his guidance and encouragement this project has become a book.

In addition, Pat Edwards of *Groundwaters* Publishing, did the formatting, covers, some editing and the placement of pictures in the text. Her help was invaluable.

Laura Wilt, librarian for ODOT, scanned most of the pictures I used in this book. She also helped clear up thorny questions in connection with the highway. With her help I was able to re-search ODOT's voluminous records. I couldn't have put this book together with out her guidance.

Then there were the museum's that generously contributed pictures and information: Clatsop County Historical Society in Astoria; Liz Johnson at Cannon Beach History Center; Mark Beach of Nehalem History Museum for his photographs; Ruby Fry-Matson from the Tillamook Museum; and Judy Knox with Bandon's Historical Museum.

Then, I received help from the University of Oregon Micro-film department, the University's Knight Library and its Ar-chives.

I would also like to thank my wife who continues to offer support.

Table of Contents

Introduction

When I give talks about my first book, *Lifting Oregon Out of The Mud* and *Building the Oregon Coast Highway*, I am asked many questions. The one that I am asked most is how I came up with the idea to write the book?

I first became curious about the Oregon Coast Highway when I learned that it had originally been called the Roosevelt Highway. After I started researching, I stumbled onto the intriguing story, one of America's great construction projects.

1925 Covered Bridge on the Roosevelt Highway

Neahkahnie

I ended the first book with the construction of the coast's five major bridges in 1936, which concluded the first phase of building Oregon's Coast Highway.

Another question I am asked is about the cliffhanging highway cutting across Neahkahnie Mountain in Oswald West State Park. People want to know more about this engineering marvel. I did too.

While researching Neakahnie I stumbled upon another story every bit as compelling as my first book. It was the story of the engineering challenges that came with the development of Oregon's spectacular coast highway in the years between Bandon's devastating fire in 1936 and the opening of the Astoria-Megler Bridge in 1966.

Disaster and Triumph

1937 Map of Oregon's Coastline
Bandon to Newport

The Astoria-Megler Bridge would not span the Columbia River for another 30 years, finally completing Oregon's Coast Highway, but when the Yaquina Bay Bridge at Newport opened in 1936, crowds turned out to celebrate. It signaled the completion of five major bridges and the ending of tedious waiting lines of the coast ferry system. The grand dedication ceremony for the Yaquina Bay Bridge was scheduled for October 3, 1936.

Tourists could hardly wait to drive across the bridge on Oregon's newly completed highway. The lazy days of summer slipped by, and the last days of September stayed hot and suffocating, instead of bringing customary rain. The warm weather spread over Oregon's southwestern counties of Lane, Douglas, Curry and Coos like a malignant shroud.

As early as September 24th the *Coos Bay Times* reported, "Fires Burning on Many Fronts in Coos Territory." Then on Saturday 26th their headline blazed, "Hot East Wind Dries Out Forest Areas." People coming from the Redwoods in northern California were met with sporadic fires out of control on both sides of the highway. People driving west from Roseburg to Coos Bay found the road even more dangerous with smoldering limbs and flaming trees falling across the road.

Fires were springing up all over southwestern Oregon. Men were recruited to fight them from logging camps, CCC units, the military, Forest Service crews, and local towns. It seemed as if all of Coos and Curry counties were ablaze.

North of Florence

2nd Street after the 1936 Bandon fire

Then the climax to these horrible fires struck on a Saturday evening, September 26, between the hours of 10 p.m. and 2 a.m. One of Oregon's most devastating fires roared through the city of Bandon. Basically nothing was left except for a few houses

Queen Anne remains after 1936 Bandon fire

Breuer Building

The First National Bank. *Bandon Museum Collection*

Bank of Bandon

Grace (Conn) Lawson & 3 children, Dollie, Harry III & Fritz

A burned-out car. *Dunshee and Stephenson Collection*

The Westland Hotel and the Moose Lodge. *Bandon Museum Collection*

Arched Doorway to Westland Hotel Otto Brewers Clothing store

Hartman Theater -Bank Of Bandon Ellington Bldg.

Hartman Theater. *Bandon Museum Collection*

Main Street ,Bandon. On the right is the Hartman Theater Flat Iron Bank Building. In the backround is the Ellingson Building

Burned out cars, logs and driftwood on beach following fire

First step in the demolition of the Bank of Bandon as part of clean-up

and businesses on the North end of town. Dow Beckham, in his book, *Bandon by the Sea*, tallied the death count at thirteen.

Some people blamed the destruction of the town on unattended, smoldering slash fires that had sent dangerous sparks into the air. Other people pointed to the unprecedented low humidity, the east winds that had dried everything out, arsonists, or the highly inflammable gorse plants. Gorse had been introduced from Ireland to plant as decorative hedges and grew in many parts of Bandon. Once the fire touched the oily plants they exploded.

The fires took their toll on forests from California to as far north as Lincoln City. Fires roared to the outskirts of coastal cities and were beaten back, or changed direction because of the wind. Parts of the Coast Highway were temporarily closed because wooden bridges had burned.

As to the severity of conditions a *Coos Bay Times* column on the 29th of September wrote about what George Turner, detective at Portland Police Department, encountered on the Coast Highway from California to Taft (now Lincoln City). He said it was smoky the entire way up the coast. "We arrived in Bandon Sunday morning— it was terrible. There was hardly a thing left…. The smoke was so thick that we had to use the lights on the car most of the way up the coast…. In a couple of places we drove between the fires burning on either side of the highway. It is just one continual fire all the way up—it looked like the end of the world."

Back in Bandon distraught people huddled on the beaches, on boats in the middle of the Coquille River, on the north spit across from town, and on the Coast Highway headed east to the town of Coquille. Bandon sent up black clouds of smoke. The residents' blackened faces told the horror they had witnessed.

After news reports spread of the devastating Bandon fire, aid began pouring in from Oregon and across the nation. Trucks filled with tents, food, and supplies, rumbled across the Coast

Fishing Fleet in Coos Bay

Range to the Coast Highway. Lingering road hazards were cleared so trucks could reach the stricken city. Money was sent too. The people of Bandon announced they were determined to rebuild.

As Dow Beckham wrote, "The courage, adaptability, and determination to rise above almost unsurmountable situations fueled the energy of hundreds to rebuild their homes, community and lives."

Marshfield waterfront

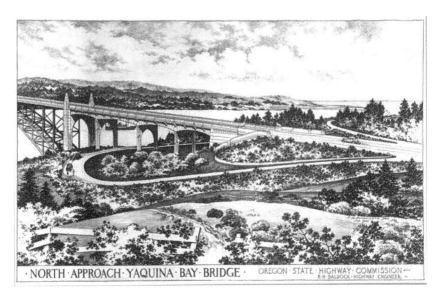

·NORTH·APPROACH·YAQUINA·BAY·BRIDGE· OREGON·STATE·HIGHWAY·COMMISSION

·YAQUINA·BAY·BRIDGE·NEWPORT· OREGON STATE HIGHWAY COMMISSION

Yaquina Bay Bridge

10

Yaquina Bay Bridge at Newport

The underpinnings of the Yaquina Bay Bridge at Newport

Ecola Bay near Astoria

While all of this was happening, preparations were being made for the dedication ceremony of the newly constructed Newport Bridge over 100 miles to the north. The day before the ceremony the *Coos Bay Times* wrote that because of the "insistence of friends along the southern Oregon Coast that the Yaquina Bay Bridge dedication…not be postponed because of fires…the celebration will take place." The Coast Guard patrol boat Pulaski from Coos Bay was scheduled to be at the ceremony. "All roads are open now to Newport."

During the dedication ceremony there were parades with military bands marching on the highway and bridge. From the bridge with its famous 600-foot steel arch, the marchers could see the naval vessels 238 feet below and the Coast Guard ship Pulaski in the bay. It was a thoroughly festive day. Former chairman of the Oregon Highway Commission, Leslie M. Scott, officially dedicated the bridge to the public.

The entire cost of the Coast Highway including the bridges according to highway department records was $25,127,572. Of this amount $8,030,285 came from the federal government. The people of Oregon had contributed the rest. Not only that, the highway and the bridges had kept Oregonians working during the tumultuous Depression years. As a result Oregonians were the benefactors and the creators of one of the most scenic highways in the world. The highway had also allowed help to reach the stricken town of Bandon quickly.

Like the rebuilding of Bandon after the fire, the building of the coast highway showed how a concerted effort of people could accomplish miracles. Oregonians had built a scenic highway stretching from the California Redwoods to the mighty Columbia River.

Without the obstructions of an antiquated ferry system tourist travel would soon jump threefold. Was the highway adequate to handle the increase? On the northern Oregon coast dreams surfaced of a daring cliff road on Neahkahnie Mountain and a tunnel that would pierce Arch Cape.

Battling Roadblocks

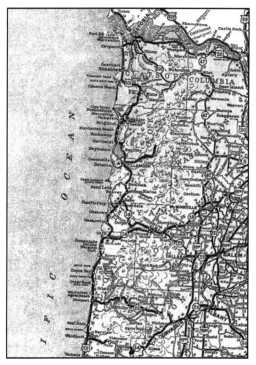

1938 Map of Oregon's Northern Coastline

In the 1930s the segment of Highway 101 between Seaside and Tillamook lurched a dozen miles inland around the east side of Neahkahnie Mountain on what is now Highway 53. The inland route was a nasty, curvy road—and still is.

Samuel Reed, a land developer in the community of Neahkahnie, wanted to straighten the road by building a new highway from Cannon Beach south along the coastline to Arch

Cape. He wanted to pierce the cape with a tunnel, veer briefly inland, and build bridges over Short Sand Beach Creek and Necarney Creek, creeks that drain into Smugglers Cove below. The road would then proceed south to

Cannon at Cannon Beach

the edge of a bluff at Neahkahnie Mountain. An early roads advocate, Reed believed a road could be built across the mountain's steep basalt face and then down its south slope to the city of Manzanita. The new road would be approximately ten miles shorter and would eliminate the dreaded curves. Reed also knew that the views from the Neahkahnie cliff road would be some of the most spectacular on the entire Oregon Coast Highway.

Southview from Neahkahnie Mountain

It was a daring idea—as imaginative as Samuel Lancaster's spectacular Columbia Gorge Highway. But the Neahkahnie site was different and even more difficult. Don Berry's novel *Trask* gives an idea of how treacherous the mountain was. In that book a young Indian guide plummets hundreds of feet to his death off the high cliff trail. Later daring men on horseback carried mail, from Seaside to Nehalem and Tillamook. Oswald West, Oregon's fourteenth governor, got the idea to set aside Oregon's beaches for public use while riding his horse "Fred The Freak" on this trail with its amazing ocean views. The old mail route on Neahkahnie Mountain has many stories of people barely escaping death.

Neahkahnie Mountain is a basalt headland that rises 1680 feet almost directly above the sea. The part that Mr. Reed wanted to build his road on was essentially a sheer cliff. His idea was to blast out a rock ledge some 600 to700 feet above crashing waves. One of the first supporters of his idea may well have

been Governor Oswald West in 1914. Simon Benson, State Highway Commissioner, supported Reed's idea in 1917, but was unable to fund it. In 1917 and 1925 Reed himself made attempts to gouge out a road. But he lacked the finances to finish the job.

Finally in October of 1930, after extensive lobbying by the people of Clatsop

Cannon Beach

and Tillamook

Cannon Beach

Counties, the State Highway Commission took over the job of building the Neahkahnie road. They planned on making it a part of the Roosevelt Highway, as the Coast highway was still called. The road would go south along the Pacific shoreline from Cannon Beach 12 miles to Manzanita.

Sam Reed was nearly 60 years old and had spent a good part of his life advocating construction of this road. He was born in Rockland, Massachusetts in 1872. In 1894 he graduated from the Massachusetts Institute of Technology. In 1902 he married Beulah Kendal and moved to Portland where they would have three daughters. In Portland, Reed assumed the duties of treasurer of the Portland Railway, Light, and Power Company. Later he worked for the Oregon Trust and Savings Bank and was elected president of Portland's Chamber Commerce. Early in his career Reed spoke out about building roads for the newly introduced automobile. He proposed to the chamber's board of trustees a 50-mile road from Portland to the coast. His proposal was rejected as impractical and expensive.

Meanwhile in 1907 Reed purchased 800 acres on Neahkahnie Mountain's ocean shore and southern slope. He subdivided and platted a portion of it. On one of the lots Reed and his wife built a cottage. They moved there in 1911. He had hoped that with the arrival of the new railway from Portland to Tillamook, in 1911, his land sales would take off. He even had a fancy brochure made up that included scenic photos.

In 1912 Reed asked fellow MIT alumnus Fuller Ellis Lawrence to design a 20-room hotel so that Reed could entertain potential land buyers. The hotel opened as the Neahkahnie Tavern and became a landmark for decades, sporting a gracious exterior with rustic shingles and a massive stone fireplace.

After a stint in the Navy during World War I, Reed returned to Neahkahnie where he became a Tillamook county commissioner in 1921. In 1931 Sam Reed watched as the highway

The Reed family's Neahkahnie Tavern. *Photo provided by Mark Beach*

Hug Point, Arch Cape, Oregon Coast Highway, Clatsop County

Neahkahnie Mountain in background

Gouging out a highway on the face of Neahkahnie

Cape Lookout

Pacific City

The Sea Stacks

commission finally started work on the northern part of the gap south of Cannon Beach. The new graveled road extended approximately three and one half miles to Hug Point. In October of 1932 the graveled road was extended another one and a half miles to Arch Cape. The gap between the two cities was narrowed farther when a section of road was built from Manzanita north and onto the southern slope of Neahkahnie Mountain.

That same year Reed became a member of the Tillamook Chamber of Commerce and by June, was an active member in the Oregon Coast Highway Association— a group of coast businessmen advocating coast highway improvements. Reed used his new position to lobby the State Highway Commission for his dream road. In September of 1933 crews built north from Manzanita to the edge of Neahkahnie's famous rock face. He must have been relieved that the roads from Cannon Beach and Manzanita were underway.

At the same time the state highway department was building two highways from Portland that would create a grand coastal loop connecting Portland with Cannon Beach and Tillamook. Reed had proposed the northern link from Portland, the Wolf Creek Highway, twenty-six years earlier. Now it is known as Highway 26. The southern link, the Wilson River Highway (now Highway 6), was to cross the Coast Range from Banks to Tillamook. Both of these roads competed for available funding with the Neahkahnie route. In August of 1934 the *Tillamook Herald* reported that $175,000 of Federal Highway Aid funds went to the Wolf Creek Highway, $42,000 to the Wilson River Highway and only $28,000 to the Neahkahnie Mountain route. All three roads were promoted as projects to provide jobs in the Depression. The new roads would also provide a much shorter driving route from Portland to the coast than the only previous option, along the banks of the Columbia River to Astoria and then south.

Sam Reed followed closely the construction of a rough road across the face of Neahkahnie Mountain. It was little more than

The Reed family

a track, but in February of 1935 workers continued north, rough-ing out a route from Neahkahnie Mountain to Necarney Creek. The gap between Manzanita and Cannon Beach was getting shorter.

Neahkahnie Mountain Section

Making cut in
Neahkahnie Mountain,
Tillamook County, 1940s

At the northern end of the gap, the road had been graveled to
Arch Cape from Cannon Beach. Instead of going over the Cape
or around to the east, the Highway Commission decided to go
through it. On March 6, 1936 the State Highway Commission
awarded a contract to the Orino, Birkemeier, and Saremal Com-

End of the parapet wall, Neahkahnie Mountain, 1940

pany to build a tunnel. Some of the tunnel funds were used to improve the rock road from Cannon Beach so heavy log trailers, trucks and shovels, could use it. The contract specified that the tunnel was to be 14'3" wide, 26' high, and 1228' long.

The highway department set the tunnel's completion for December 31, 1936, but that date proved to be impossibly optimistic, and the tunnel wouldn't be fully completed until March of 1940. Countless difficulties led to the embarrassing delay. Crumbly sandstone at both entrances required extra timber reinforcement to prevent cave-ins. Once the men reached the

Building of the Arch Cape Tunnel

The Building of the
Arch Cape Tunnel

25

Arch Cape Tunnel

The building of the "The Tunnel" at Cannon Beach, Oregon.
Photo by Haworthy from the Cannon Beach Museum

basalt portion in the center of the tunnel, they made good progress. However, working in the winter months was extremely difficult for gas-powered shovels and trucks. Mud was so deep that gas donkeys were required to pull out stuck vehicles.

"Heavy rains, mud, inexperienced supervision and tunnel men, improper equipment," and trouble in getting supplies caused the delays, according to a report written by an Oregon State Highway Department cost analyst E.H. Clymer. Clymer concluded that the big losers were the contractors.

It was both dangerous and taxing work. One man quit his job because he could not tolerate the carbon monoxide fumes inside the tunnel. Clymer supports that claim by writing on September 15, 1937 "… the crew is working in gas fumes due to lack of ventilation system, which decreases efficiency." Even though there were ventilating fans and a pipe installed to draw out the fumes, sometimes they seemed inefficient. After tunnel men abruptly quit, others quickly filled their spot. Jobs were scarce.

Mr. Charles E. Haddix filled one of these vacancies and later wrote about his experience in the *Arch Cape Chronicles*. "Severe headaches from the carbon monoxide gasses inside the tunnel caused some men to quit. I managed to last three months. Then, one night I backed into a hole on the fill where I was unloading and as I attempted to pull out, I snapped the left rear axle on my truck. The short-fused foreman was nearby so I happened to be on the receiving end of his wrath that night and lost my job."

Meanwhile Sam Reed had become one of three vice presidents for the Oregon Coast Highway Association. Along with his new administration duties he also kept watch on the progress of the Necarney section of road. He was probably on hand in December of 1936 when road crews reached the banks of

Neahkahnie Mountain Section, 1940

Necarney Creek. The road from Manzanita across the face of Neahkahnie Mountain was still very rough, but it allowed crews to bring in the heavy equipment and the steel girders necessary for the construction of the Necarney Creek Bridge.

On April 2, 1937, an article in the *North Tillamook County News* reported, "The first steel on the bridge across Neahkahnie Creek [Necarney Creek] began Wednesday of this week." In June enough of the bridge was completed so that work could be started building the road north to Short Sand Beach Creek, approximately one quarter of a mile. When that road was complete they would start building the smaller Short Sand Creek Bridge. Reed continually informed the Highway Association of progress. The Association routinely met in different locations along the coast from Astoria to Coos Bay. Their widely circulated minutes were reported in newspapers all over the state; summarizing progress on all coast projects and offering new promotional ideas inviting tourists to Oregon.

A staff writer for the *Oregonian*, Herbert Lundy, wanted to find out just how much progress had been made on Neahkahnie

Arch Cape Tunnel in progress

Masonry retaining wall, Neahkahnie Mountain, 1940s

Neahkahnie Mountain, 1940s

Mountain. He wrote in May of 1937, "The road to Neah-Kah-nie leaves the present coast highway between Wheeler and Mohler, runs through the old fishing town of Nehalem, misses Manzanita's long beach by a quarter mile, and curves up Classic Ridge before it slants upward onto the face of the mountain... It is possible now to drive from Nehalem north on the new road only to the concrete bridge being erected over the Short Sand Creek, and from Cannon Beach south only to the tunnel being drilled through the rock at Arch Cape."

If he actually drove north from Nehalem his trip must have been a little frightening. He would have had to drive on the narrow cliff of Neahkahnie's western face, with its uncompleted

The Arch Cape Tunnel

viaducts, no guardrails, and a road strewn with rocks and heavy road building equipment. He would have had to cross over the old wooden Chasm Bridge, then cross the Necarney Creek Bridge still under construction, in order to reach Short Sand Beach Creek Bridge. The workmen must have been off that day. Lundy mentions nothing about such hardships.

The *Astoria Evening Budget* reported in July 1937, that $620,000 was still needed to be spent to finish the nine and a half miles of roadways separating Hug Point from Manzanita.

The worst and most undeveloped part of this stretch was be-tween Arch Cape tunnel and Short Sand Creek Bridge—a dis-tance of about 3 miles. This connecting piece of road still needed clearing, building, grading, and surfacing. In August a contract was signed for the clearing work.

The Oregon Coast Highway Association must have been pleased with the completion of the Necarney Creek Bridge in September 1937, closing another gap around the mountain. But then at a meeting in October of 1937 the Coast Association launched a new idea — a new coast route between Barview (north of Tillamook) southward to Pacific City. It would have been a major relocation of the highway from its inland route, and included a new stretch of road along the coastline for approxi-mately 25 miles. It also necessitated a new bridge over Tillamook Bay. Henry F. Cabell, Chairman of the State Highway Commission was quick to quell the Association's enthusiasm by reminding them of huge expenditures on roads still unfinished, including the one at Neahkahnie Mountain. The association quickly tabled the motion, calling instead for the immediate completion of the Neahkahnie-Cannon Beach section of the Coast Highway.

In the first days of November 1937, an engineer named William Saremal boasted that cars could be driven through the Arch Cape tunnel. An article in the *Evening Astoria Budget* claimed the only other work needed on the tunnel was "construc-tion of the pavement and the sidewalks." On this date, however, there was no road at all south of the tunnel. A few months later the *Oregon Journal* reported that "the new highway work ends in a maze of heavy timber and deep canyons." If the tunnel was indeed finished it was a tunnel to nowhere.

On the other end of that rugged three-mile gap, stood the newly completed Short Sand Beach Creek Bridge. It was fin-ished on November 10, 1937 at a cost of $10, 979.

The *North Tillamook County News*, praised Sam Reed in July 1938 as the man "whose vision and boosting the past 25 years are largely responsible for the construction of the sightly bridge (Necarney Bridge) and of the scenic highway around Neahkahnie Mountain." The next month the Necarney Creek Bridge was dedicated to Samuel G. Reed. It had cost $79,000 to build. Also in August the contract was awarded to grade the final stretch of highway between Short Sand Creek Bridge and Arch Cape Tunnel.

For decades Sam Reed had worked for his dream road across Neahkahnie Mountain—a dream that many thought was impossible. He had rattled cages, roared at the western gales, shaken people's hands, led organizations, and even donated 97 acres of his mountain property so the Highway Commission could build the road. Reed also sold another 239 acres to the parks department, which was part of the Highway Commission at that time.

The new Short Sand Creek Bridge was nothing elegant. Its three spans of reinforced concrete deck girder had minimal detail, although the railings had floral paneling. The nearby

SHORT · SAND · BEACH · CREEK · BRIDGE

Short Sand Beach Creek Bridge. *Oregon State Highway Commission. Drawing by F.G. Hutchinson, '37*

Necarney Creek Bridge had a grade of nearly 6 per cent, and included a curve that weaved into the surrounding mountainous terrain. Six green steel trestle towers supported a road of steel girders 85 feet above the creek bed. The bridge was surfaced with concrete, and included sidewalks and gothic railings. It blended in so well with the mountainous landscape that travelers often did not notice they were traveling high above a creek.

Six hundred spectators came to see the dedication ceremony for the two new bridges that day. A band played and people danced on the surfaces of the shiny new spans. Speakers included Tillamook and Clatsop County commissioners, and former Oregon Highway Chairman Leslie M. Scott. Even C. B.

Setting first column of the Necarney Creek Bridge, April 16, 1937

Construction of the
Necarney Creek Bridge

The Necarney Creek
Bridge Construction

Necarney Creek Bridge Construction

McCullough and Glenn Paxson, prestigious bridge engineers for the state highway department, were on hand to praise Reed for his contributions in time and leadership. At the end of the ceremony Boy Scouts lifted the veil on the bridge plaque that read:

Neahkahnie Creek Bridge

Dedicated to Samuel G. Reed
In Recognition of The Years of Service
Given by Him To The
Development Of Oregon Highways
August 28, 1938

It had taken Reed nearly thirty years to reach this point. His dream of a finished road was at last in sight. He was 66 years old. His wife Beulah, one of the last speakers said, "I don't know what Sam will do for a hobby when the road is finished. He has visited the construction camps every day for many years."

Dedication cememony for the opening of the Necarney Creek Bridge, August 28, 1938. *Photo provided by Mark Beach*

But Sam Reed's road was not yet complete...

Cliffhanging Highway

Storms were common in Cannon Beach while building the highway -
1939 storm at Cannon Beach

Logs and debris had to be cleaned up in the Cannon Beach
storm of 1939

Two months after the Necarney Creek Bridge was dedicated in his honor, Sam Reed was elected President of the Oregon Coast Highway Association. He used the new position to push even harder for the completion of the road. The association knew that completion of the grand coastal loop from Portland would increase tourist travel and raise property values significantly. The Wolf Creek Highway and the Wilson River Highway were proceeding slowly. By midyear 1939 major portions of each highway still needed work. They needed a tunnel and three bridges—The Nehalem River Bridge, the Quartz Creek Bridge, the Devils Fork Bridge.

Nehalem River Bridge, Wolf Creek Highway.
Drawing by F.G. Hutchinson, '37

The Nehalem River Bridge, just east of the community of Elsie, promised to be another one of Oregon's great bridges, featuring a graceful 231-foot reinforced-concrete deck arch. Its railings and decorative details recalled the scenic bridges of the Columbia River Gorge Highway and many on the Oregon Coast. Three miles to the southeast, the Quartz Creek Bridge, resembled the elegant but practical Sam Reed Bridge. The *North Tillamook County News*, wrote in July 39, "A notable engineering achievement." Further east, closer to Portland there were plans to build a tunnel.

Recurring forest fires hampered construction of these inland highways. The great Tillamook Burn of 1933 still scarred the terrain, with 240,000 acres of scorched snags. In 1939 another fire burned off some that had escaped the first fire. Some of the road and bridge building crews were called in to fight the fires.

The bridges were all built under the supervision of the Oregon state bridge engineer, Glen Paxson. An Oregonian by birth, he graduated from Oregon State College with a Bachelor of Science degree in 1912. He was appointed bridge engineer in 1935, replacing Conde B. McCullough, who had been loaned to the Public Roads Administration to handle structures on the Inter-American Highway in Central America. Paxson would supervise bridges all over Oregon. Among Paxson's hobbies were a penchant for math and a love of baseball statistics. Perhaps as a result, he designed the lofty bridges in the Coast Range and those on Reed's Neahkahnie Mountain with a mathematician's zeal. They were also appealing to the eye and matched the landscape well.

In September of 1939 the final contract was signed on Arch Cape Tunnel—the paving and lining. Meanwhile the Oregon State Highway Commission began the final work on the Neahkahnie Mountain road. They signed a contract with a Seattle firm, the K. L. Goulter's Construction Company, on December 8, 1939, to build a chasm bridge, several half viaducts, and rock walls along the face of the mountain. The con-

Building the Chasm Bridge on Neakahnie Mountain - 1941

Building the Chasm Bridge on Neakahnie Mountain - 1941

Building the Chasm Bridge on Neakahnie Mountain - 1941

tract also included the final grading and surfacing of the highway from the Necarney Creek Bridge south to Manzanita.

The Seattle construction company first had to build housing for the hundreds of workers the job would require—four bunkhouses, a bathhouse, a mess hall, and buildings for equipment. As the men worked, the steep basalt cliffs towered above them, and waves crashed on rocks 500 feet below. The workers used native rock whenever possible for the retaining walls and para-

The completed Chasm Bridge

pet. The resulting rockwork remains historically significant, because masonry of this sort was used only prior to the Second World War. The specific people or ethnic group who did the stonework on Neahkahnie Mountain was not recorded. It is highly possible that Italian immigrants did it since they did other stonework on the highways and parks of Oregon.

Not all of Sam Reed's thoughts were on road construction during this time. Just before Christmas 1939 he learned that a 14-year-old blind girl from Garibaldi needed a typewriter. The *North Tillamook County News* reported that he donated his own typewriter to the young girl, and she immediately began writing stories.

The finished Arch Cape tunnel.
Photo courtesy of the Cannon Beach Museum

By March of 1940 Arch Cape Tunnel was finally completed at a total cost of $287, 000. In October, Henry Kern of North Bend succeeded Sam Reed as President of the Coast Highway Association.

That November roving reporter Fred T. Mellinger of the *Tillamook Herald* responded to an "…urgent invitation to visit the construction site work on Neh-Kah-Nie Mountain…." He reported that he "finally reached the end of the traveled road and pulled out on a wide parking space…. The road has been widened and for a mile or more workmen have constructed an ornamental rock wall some 18 or more inches in width that will protect the motorist from running off the bluff. Another thing that attracted our attention, is what the workmen told us was a half bridge. These are constructed at points where fills are impossible or impracticable, but which now will make a safe highway.

"We were fortunate in arriving just in time to see workmen climbing back up ropes to the highway, after they had hung

Neahkahnie Mountain Segment

Outside parapet wall

precariously over the sides of the wall preparing a face shot, which was fired while we at the safe distance watched the tons of rock that were blown from the side of the mountain in preparations for making footings for another of the half bridges... When completed it will be one of nature's rich spots for tourists."

Finally, after eight years of construction work, the official opening of the grand Neahkahnie road was scheduled for Sunday August 3, 1941. That date should have been a triumph for Samuel G. Reed, the 69-year-old, proprietor of the Neahkahnie Tavern who had fought so long and hard to see the road completed. But a heart attack killed Reed on July 22, 1941 just twelve days before the celebration. In his obituary The *Tillamook Herald* wrote, "his pet project was the Neahkahnie shortcut." The *Seaside Signal* added, "Sam could not live to see the final completion of a dream that had guided the major portion of his adult life—the highway over Neah-Kah-Nie Mountain."

And so Reed was not among the more than three thousand people who attended the opening ceremonies. The road wasn't completely finished, but it was far enough along to hold the event. Parts of the highway still needing oiling, and a few segments were blocked off. Many of the celebration's attendees crossed, and then re-crossed the shiny steel-towered Samuel G. Reed Bridge. They did double takes off Neahkahnie's bluff. From there they looked hundreds of feet down, to the south, and saw Reed's famous Neahkahnie Tavern, snugly set on the edge of the Pacific Ocean. The *Seaside Signal* reported, "residents of the district served 1300 pounds of barbequed salmon and gallons of soft drinks... Music was provided by the Seaside Girls band."

People hiked down from the new road to Smugglers Cove and Short Sand Beach. They gasped as they drove around the mountain on the perilous cliff-hanging highway, perhaps the most spectacular section of the Oregon Coast Highway. It was lined with ornamental stonework and ocean vistas in a setting of preserved forestlands. The *Oregonian* described the new route

New masonry retaining wall, Neahkahnie Mountain

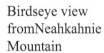

Birdseye view fromNeahkahnie Mountain

between Manzanita and Cannon Beach along the face of the Neahkahnie Mountain as, "possibly the most scenic drive in the world." It was a road hewn from a cliff, like none other.

As for the Wilson River Highway, and the Wolf Creek Highway both of these connecting routes from Portland were delayed by the declaration of war in December 1941 and would not officially open until October of 1948. The total price tag for them topped ten million dollars.

The Wilson River Highway became U.S. 6, and the Wolf Creek Highway became U.S. Highway 26. Oregon added the name Sunset Highway in August of 1947 in honor of the men who served in Oregon's famous 41st Sunset Division during World War II.

This photo shows inclination of rock sloping towards the future wall. This inclined plane is found beneath each layer

Neahkahnie Mountain was now just 80 miles from Portland via the Sunset Highway. State Parks director Samuel Boardman began buying property to preserve 2500 acres of the scenic coast between Neahkahnie Mountain and Arch Cape as a park. Boardman admitted that the 436 acres Samuel Reed had sold or donated to the state of Oregon, included, "the most scenic parts of the park—that scenic overlook where parking turnouts have been provided and east of the highway taking in a goodly portion of the western slope of the mountain.... It would be difficult to place the actual valuation on this property for it is the scenic window of our coastline."

In May of 1958 Short Sand Beach State Park's name was changed to honor Oswald West, Oregon's fourteenth Governor. West wrote the legislation in 1913 that set Oregon's beaches aside for public use, and the park remains a fitting tribute to Oregon's rascally one-term governor. Both Governor West and Samuel Reed were early road advocates. Now they will forever be immortalized on Neahkanie Mountain. One could almost say

View from newly completed Neahkahnie Mountain road

that when Samuel G. Reed passed away in 1941 he bequeathed to the State of Oregon the Neahkahnie Mountain road—then a new segment of the Oregon Coast Highway.

New route of Oregon Coast Highway on Neahkahnie Mountain in Tillamook County, 1941-1942

Depoe Bay

1937 Map of the Oregon Coast Highway near Depot Bay

The Oregon Coast Highway over Neahkahnie Mountain was a unique addition to the highway. Another unique addition happened when Conde B. McCullough designed the first arched bridge on Oregon's coast—at Depoe Bay in 1927. Its design would be copied extensively in bridges from Rocky Creek Bridge in the north to the I. A. Patterson Bridge at Gold Beach in the south—where not one, but multiple arches skimmed across

Patterson Bridge at the mouth of the Rogue River

the Rogue River supporting the road above. Other coast bridges would include variations, with the roadway through the steel arch, as was built in Yaquina Bay and with the roadway through the concrete arch, like the Big Creek Bridge between Florence and Yachats.

Since the Depoe Bay Bridge was McCullough's first reinforced concrete arch bridge on the coast, it was significant. Because of this bridge and the arched bridges built in the ensuing years, Oregon's Coast Highway became one of the most scenic in the world. Who would have thought that from Oregon's smallest harbor, possibly the world's smallest harbor, so many exciting and architecturally pleasing arched bridges would follow.

Depoe Bay was named after Charlie Depoe, a Siletz Indian. His tribe and descendants had gained ownership of the Depoe Bay area from the federal government. Then they sold their land to a land developer around 1926-27. The company platted the land into small residential lots and sold them for $100 each. The developers thought with the building of a bridge, and its connection with the Oregon Coast Highway, there would be a steady stream of potential buyers. This type of land speculation was common in the early 20th century. Much like Samuel Reed and

Depoe Bay

his purchase of land around Neahkahnie Mountain. With the Depoe Bay Bridge the traveler coming from Newport could now travel unobstructed across the new bridge and reach Kernville and Taft to the north.

For coastal communities Depoe Bay got off to a slow start. Most coastal communities had already incorporated. Since the adjoining land was still in the developmental stage the bridge was more of a highway extension than an adjunct for city commerce. The bridge would span the treacherous entry into the little harbor. Locals referred to entering the bay as "shooting the hole." The bridge was 312 feet long with a 150-foot single span reinforced-concrete arch. It was only 18 feet wide and had no sidewalks. The cost of the bridge was $55,000. Despite its narrow lanes and lack of sidewalks, the bridge became a popular haven for sightseers. They wanted to see fishing boats navigate through the bay's narrow inlet.

A few miles to the south another similar bridge was under construction—the Rocky Creek Bridge. It was dedicated on

September 17, 1927, just three months after the first Depoe Bay Bridge. But Rocky Creek was longer, at 360 feet, having a central arch of 160 feet, and a roadway width of 20 feet. It looked almost identical to the Depoe Bay Bridge; still, it lacked the attraction of a harbor below.

A division of the Oregon State Highway Commission had the responsibility of promoting Oregon tourism. Since Oregon's

Roosevelt Coast Highway crossing of Rocky Creek, 10 miles north of Newport

Elk at Delake

Depoe Bay charter

coast was one of the most scenic spots in Oregon many photographs were taken of it. These were sent to state and national media—newspapers and popular magazines. Tourists began to flock to Oregon's coast. One popular haven was Depoe Bay. Tourists wanted to see the spouting horn, the whales, and the captains piloting their boats through the narrow inlet. So many tourists came that they became a traffic hazard on the narrow bridge. By 1939 something had to be done.

The highway commission and bridge department, under Paxson, came to the conclusion that the bridge and roadway had to be widened to 48 feet plus five-foot sidewalks. The improvement would also include a walkway under the north end of the structure which made it possible for pedestrians to cross from the business section on the east side of the highway to the state park on the west side without danger. It was decided that by constructing an additional arch immediately west of the existing two 150-foot single span reinforced-concrete deck arches, it

Depoe Bay

Depoe Bay

would allow for the necessary widening of the bridge. When it was completed hardly anyone noticed that the construction of the Depoe Bay Bridge had spanned more than thirteen years. The cost of the addition seemed modest for the times—completed on November 15, 1940 the cost was only $60,000. In

2005 the bridge was placed on the National Register of Historic Places.

With the completion of the Depoe Bay Bridge and the highway between Cannon Beach and Manzanita it was presumed that tourists would flock to the Oregon Coast Highway. From the banks of the Columbia River to the California border, it seemed

Yaquina Bay State Park

Alsea Bridge

Alsea Bridge

Entrance to Sea Lion Caves (circled)

Mile-long Coos Bay Bridge

the highway was really finished. The Highway Commission had its promotional department step up its advertising campaign. The exciting new bridges over bays and rivers sparkled. The prolonged drought that had plagued the forests with devastating forest fires at Bandon and Tillamook, and even threatened traffic on the coast highway, seemed at an end. That drought from 1928 to 1941 had been one of the worst on record.

Commerce was picking up too, especially lumber with log trucks whizzing over the new road. In 1938 Oregon became the largest producer of lumber in the United States. Trucks over 50 feet in length had to obtain new operating permits from the county and state. Accountants from the highway department eagerly counted more monies coming into the state from permits and gas taxes. People were employed building highways—Wolf Creek, Wilson River, and others. Roads from the inland valleys to the coast were rapidly being improved and completed. Oregon had successfully pulled itself out of the Great Depression. Free accessible beaches beckoned. The *Oregonian* wrote in August of 1941, "The Oregon Coast highway had its heaviest travel in history during July and August."

Suddenly the enthusiasm was a distant clamor ebbing out to sea. On December 7, 1941 the Japanese bombed Pearl Harbor. The United States was at war.

Highway signs of the 1940s

War Years

As early as February 1941, State Highway Engineer R. H. Baldock wrote that highways were built for the economic needs of citizens, but also functioned as roads to military forts, airports, and munitions dumps. In the event the U.S. was drawn into the European conflict Oregon's roads had to be built to withstand army convoy trucks and shipments of military weapons. They would also have to withstand the heavy use of logging trucks, because wood was an indispensible commodity in planes, boats, and other war necessities.

Anticipating war Baldock wrote that western states needed a bigger share of federal highway allocations. It made sense, since Oregon's shores might be invaded first. If war did come Oregon's Coast Highway would be indispensible.

The idea of Oregon's Coast Highway as a military route was not a new one. In 1917 a state senator proposed a petition to the Oregon State Legislature urging Congress to build a defensive highway.

"The people of the Pacific Coast States," Smith's petition stated, "urgently request the building and maintaining of a military highway along the Pacific Coast from the Canadian border to the Mexican border for military necessities and defense such as supplying coast forts with guns and ammunition, the handling of artillery, ammunition and mobilizing troops in the event of an invasion."

While the highway was under construction from 1921-1931 it was called the Roosevelt Military Highway. Sometime between those dates the word "military" was dropped, and the road became known as the Roosevelt Highway. In 1931 the state legislature changed the name to the Oregon Coast Highway. In 1941, 24 years after I. S. Smith's petition, Oregon's Coast Highway was about to become a real military highway.

Oregon's state highway engineer Baldock's defensive plan had three points: 1) "Replacement of narrow or weak bridges... 2) Elimination of bottlenecks... and, 3) Widening of congested sections of routes through cities." Oregon's Republican United States Senator Rufus C. Holman, a member of the Senate military affairs commission said he had "concern over the possibility of invasion of the Pacific Coast. I cannot go into detail because of the nature of the information I received. But I can say that our army and navy strategists have given thorough consideration to this entire problem and that they have made and are making such disposition of armed forces, and providing defense measures as in their judgment seem best calculated to protect the lives and homes of our western people." One newspaper reported that hidden in the northwest forests of the United States were airfields and munitions dumps. Senator Charles L. McNary said, "Oregon probably will get more funds under an allocation based strictly on defense needs."

As the United States drew closer to war, Governor Charles A. Sprague formed the Oregon Defense Council in June of 1941. The defense council provided the framework for enlisting civilian volunteers to meet the threat of enemy attack. None too soon, because on December 7, Pearl Harbor was bombed. With the threat of an invasion Sprague's ODC suddenly caught people's attention. Hordes of civilians signed up for the plan, including women, men too young for enlistment, and men too old. They staffed observation posts in fire lookouts and observation buildings all over Oregon. Many were part of the Aircraft Warning Service, which kept vigil against unauthorized planes. A majority of these lookouts were built in the Coast Range mountains.

Ecola State Park

In December of 1941 the *Cohassett Beach Chronicles* wrote that "a remarkable fleet of military and private planes and boats of all kinds was commandeered by the Army and Coast Guard to patrol the western shoreline." Observation and reconnaissance missions by trained and untrained pilots flew above Oregon's beaches keeping watch. Military and Coast Guard personnel were positioned at strategic spots on the Oregon coast.

These efforts, as uncoordinated as they were, were successful. Lying off the coast of Oregon were two Japanese submarines, the I-26 and I-25, both equipped with planes that could be catapulted from their decks. They had originally been ordered to bomb Oregon Coast cities on Christmas. The vigilance of Oregon's civilian and armed forces on the Pacific coast kept them under water. Soon Japan's plan of attack was scrapped. Their submarines returned home.

The fear of an attack at home gripped the United States. High-ranking military leaders on February 14, 1942 stressed the need for the evacuation of all Japanese and other suspected subversives from the Pacific Coast. They were to be moved immediately to inland relocation camps. Gas masks and stretchers were issued to those who lived in populous areas and the dangers of mustard gas and lewisite were explained. First aid courses became common. Newspapers reported information on blackouts and air raid warnings. Sirens were set up. Protocol was explained for emergencies.

Governor Charles A. Sprague reduced the maximum speed limit from 55mph to 40 mph. Two reasons prompted this action—gas and rubber. Both were to be rationed and enforced by law if necessary. New road construction was stopped, except for military needs. The Oregon Highway Commission's Fifteenth Biennial Report banned "construction projects except for.... access roads leading to military reservations and war industries or flight strips. This, presumably will spell the end of the highway construction program for the duration." Raw materials were needed for the nation's production of planes, tanks, ships and munitions. Wood was in high demand and many coast forests were leveled to satisfy the demand.

In 1942 everyone was concerned about a Japanese invasion on Oregon's beaches. Parallel to those beaches was Hwy 101. Along with the railroads, the highway provided military shipments of munitions and soldiers to the newly organized coast defenses. Shipments poured into Tongue Point Naval Air Station on the Columbia River and Fort Stevens on Oregon's northern coast. The fort included barracks for the enlisted men, mess halls, and training areas. Weapons were distributed at Battery Russell, Battery Clark, Battery Pratt, and a base near the south jetty of the Columbia River. There were nests for machine guns, and the batteries had big cannons.

Battery Russell had the best vantage point for returning fire on ocean approaches by an enemy. Not far from Fort Stevens

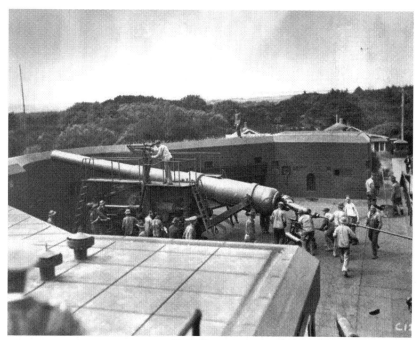

Fort Stevens

North of Tillamook Head

Gray Memorial Chapel, Clatsop County

was the mouth of the Columbia River. The Army purchased a
ferry called *Tourist No. 2* in December of 1941. *Tourist 2*'s
normal duties had been ferrying cars across the Colombia River,
connecting drivers traveling north and south on Highway 101.
But the Army had more urgent need of it. The ferryboat's big
deck was a great storage area for explosive mines. Then army
personnel laid and tended mines at the mouth of the Columbia.

On June 21, 1942, driving from Portland to the beaches for
an occasional family outing may have been difficult if not
impossible. It was going against the rationing efforts of the
country. If a family dared take the trip it would be fraught with
invasions of their privacy. The trouble was gas rationing and
rubber tires. Gas cards were needed. Regulations controlled the
use and purchase of rubber tires. There was even a ban on the
sale of new automobiles.

If a Portland family had dared to take a trip to the beach,
they would have experienced trouble getting enough gas ration-

ing cards. Then they would have had to get permission for use of car tires. If they left Portland at 5pm they might have arrived in Astoria about 7:30. If they stopped for supper at a restaurant, military personnel would have crowded the nearby tables, gas masks dangling from their belts. The soldiers' tin canisters held neutralizing substances to filter poison from the air. If a daughter to the family had pulled out her Brownie camera and taken pictures, a uniformed officer would have rushed to their table to confiscate the camera. Cameras were banned in Astoria near military posts. During dinner waiters might well have rushed into the dinning area shouting "Blackout, blackout!" All the lights would be turned off and the windows shuttered. Three hours later the lights might be turned back on. If the father asked for a cup of coffee, the waiter might have replied, "Sorry, we have used up our allotment of coffee and sugar for today."

After their cold meal the family might have travelled south to Skipanon on Highway 101. If it were June their windows would be rolled down to enjoy the ocean air. Suddenly at the intersection of Delaura Beach Road and Hwy 101 they could have heard gun blasts from the sea. A shell could have whistled in and exploded, shooting sparks everywhere. Nearby Fort Stevens' sirens would have blared. Fearing more shells the father might have sped to 50 miles an hour. Soon they would have heard a siren and seen flashing lights from behind. The police-man would have issued them a citation for speeding. The speed limit was 40 miles an hour. While driving across the mountain road at Neahkahnie Mountain the family's headlights would have shot out over the roadside embankments. But another siren would have erupted behind them. This time they would have been given a warning ticket— headlights must be dimmed. The next morning when the exhausted family arrived back in Port-land, newspaper headlines would have announced, Japanese Submarine attacks Fort Stevens.

The Japanese submarine I-25 had made the daring attack by slipping past minefields and other ships. Surfacing south of the Columbia River and offshore from Fort Steven's Battery Russell,

Ferry laying mines during World War II

the sub blasted 17 rounds from its deck gun. The blasts set off alarms sending men rushing to their battle stations. The commander of the Columbia River Defenses decided not to fire back, fearing it would give away their position. The submarine shells did little damage. Afterwards I-25 dove under the water and sped away. The day before off the coast of Washington near Fort Flattery I-25 had attacked and disabled the coal burning cargo ship S.S. Fort Camosun. All people survived both attacks. After the attack at Fort Stevens I-25 returned to Yokosuka Naval Base in Japan.

The daring attack brought to life claims from the Army, Navy, Coast Guard, and Oregon Civil Defense that Oregon had better be prepared for war. "Naval shore stations along the Pacific coast from San Diego to Puget Sound, when properly implemented with land-based bombers, sea planes and patrol blimps, will be adequate to cope with any threatened invasion," Representative James W. Mott declared in the *Oregonian* on

Tillamook High School

Tillamook dairy herd

Pacific City

Bay Ocean Natatorium ruins

August 8. And in Tillamook preparations were already underway to build two blimp hangars. The U. S. Navy had determined that lighter than air blimps could perform reconnaissance missions along Oregon's coast. The approximately 2000-acre air base had a western and southern boundary that fronted on Highway 101.

Other precautionary steps were being taken up north. The United States Coast Guard called for restricted areas in Astoria and along the Columbia River. Waterfront personnel needed identification cards, and strict rules were placed on vehicles and boats.

Dim out signs on Oregon's Coast Highway

Dim-outs were ordered by the middle of August for the entire coast. Most lights visible from the sea were banned, including billboards, marquees, windows, and car headlights. One especially bad area for car lights was in Curry County on Highway 101. The stretch of highway followed the beaches from Port Orford south to Gold Beach. Many dim-out signs had been posted. However there were many lawbreakers because at night it was hard to see the road and enforcement was rare. In the early morning hours of September 9, 1941 the Japanese Submarine I-25, about 30 miles out to sea west of Brookings, possibly observed a tranquil green Oregon coast.

They had patiently waited underwater in rough seas about a week or so for the rain and fog to clear. When it did they surfaced. From a watertight compartment on the deck the crew removed the hull of a seaplane. Next they attached wings and floats. The plane was set on an air- driven catapult and readied for launch. Its pilot, Nobuo Fujita, and navigator, Petty Officer Shoji Okuda, had orders to drop two incendiary bombs on the forest east of Brookings. Their mission was to start a forest fire.

As the little seaplane buzzed eastward over Highway 101 and Brookings in the clear morning sunshine it seemed nothing

Old Catholic Church at Cape Blanco

could stop Fujita. Numerous ground lookouts were on duty that morning. A soldier with "G" company of the 174th infantry, 44th division reported to his commanding officer Captain Claude Waldrop that he had seen a plane come in from the sea about 6am. Later it departed at 6:30. The Captain reported the news to the Roseburg Filter Center.

Captain Waldrop worried more about a ground invasion than planes because he had the job of keeping the coast safe—from Coos Bay to the California line. He had detachments of troops consisting of about 200 men stationed along the coast. His forces had outdated rifles and machine guns and the captain wondered how he could protect the coastline with so few men and such primitive weapons. Should an attack occur, it would take considerable time to move reinforcements over the winding and steep highway between Gold Beach and Brookings. He and his men came up with one idea though to confuse the enemy. They took down all the Highway 101 road signs.

At 6:24 am the little seaplane was seen about eight miles inland by a lookout on Mount Emily. He reported the strange plane to the Roseburg Filter Center too. A Coast Guardsman at Chetco Point Lookout heard the plane, along with someone at the Long Ridge Lookout. The Filter Station was to report their findings to the Information Center who would alert fighter planes to intervene. Had all gone according to plan Fujita would never have made it back to his submarine. But, a mix-up happened; either fighter planes were sent in the wrong direction or the Filter Station simply dismissed the information as irrelevant.

Fujita flew back to the I-25 submarine and landed on the ocean. The submarine's crane lifted his plane from the sea to the deck. The plane was quickly disassembled and returned to the watertight compartment. He and his co-pilot had dropped two bombs and had seen one explode. Fujita thought he had accomplished his mission—they had attacked the United States mainland, and had started a fire.

At noon the Mount Emily lookout reported a fire "five miles to the southeast." Men rushed to the location and doused it. Had

Cape Blanco

Port Orford

Knapp Hotel, Port Orford

it been 1933, (the Tillamook Burn), 1936, (Bandon's loss) or 1939, (another Tillamook Burn) Fujita's bomb may have started a conflagration. But several days of rain and fog had left the forest damp and soggy. It had simply been the wrong day, and year, for such an undertaking. So Fujita failed in his mission of starting a major forest fire.

Fujita's submarine narrowly escaped when an Army Air Force Hudson bomber happened along on an antisubmarine patrol and spotted the sub descending under the water. The bomber dropped three 300 pounds bombs over the sub's wake. The Japanese submarine was rocked around but only sustained minor damage and slipped away. It lay off the Oregon coast for about 20 days. Finally in the early morning of September 29, it surfaced approximately 60 miles north of the first bombing. The little seaplane was readied for another takeoff. Fujita and his co-pilot were catapulted into the morning darkness intent on dropping two more incendiary bombs. They sailed east and then southeast leaving Cape Blanco behind. They reached Grassy Knob, 8 miles inland from Highway 101 and Port Orford. Fujita dropped the bombs, and claimed to have seen an explosion. Observers at Grassy Knob saw the plane at 5:22 am, and saw and heard an explosion too. Then the plane circled north and west, looping past Edison Butte, approximately 10 miles inland from Cape Blanco, where the seaplane was spotted again. Fujita and his co-pilot flew on by, and returned safely to their submarine. Again they thought they had accomplished their mission. Yet the bombs were never found. Perhaps the bombs exploded but failed to ignite in a waterlogged forest.

Senator Rufus Holman asked for immediate establishment of a Pacific Coast civil air patrol in response to the shelling of Fort Stevens and the incendiary bombs that had been dropped in Curry County. The senator did not know that the I-25 submarine had sunk two cargo ships and a Soviet submarine on its way back to Japan. What Senator Holman wanted was a greater concentration of troops and patrol planes on Oregon's coast. By early 1943 that happened—Oregon's beaches were heavily patroled by the Coast Guard. Radar detection stations were set up at Tillamook Head, Oceanside, Cape Foulweather, Siletz Bay, Delake, Cape Perpetua, Cape Arago, and Cape Sebastian.

Cape Perpetua

Cape Arago

Meanwhile the U. S. Navy's blimps began arriving at the Naval Air Station in Tillamook. The first blimp K-31 arrived on February 15, 1943. Hangar B was not complete so the ship had to be moored outside. In March of 1943 a gale pulled the blimp from its mooring and smashed it to pieces not far from Highway 101. Other blimps survived and were able to perform their support roles, assisting the Coast Guard on the beaches, doing reconnaissance for submarines, and escorting ships from the Pacific into the Columbia River.

Businesses on the Coast Highway suffered during the war. They were forced to ration gas, tires, metals, and foods. Once flourishing businesses sank in debt. Just a year and a half earlier the Oregon Coast Highway had been advertised as the mecca of the tourist industry. People had invested heavily in beachside resorts and tourist attractions. Now, in March of 1943, business owners prayed for the war to end. One column in the *Oregonian* began with, "Curtains for the Coast?" The federal government threatened to end all pleasure trips and patriotically proclaimed that all rationed goods should go to the front lines first. So with gas, rubber, food rationing, higher taxes, no lights visible from the sea, cameras banned, no beach fires, no night walks on the beach, tourism vanished. It was not uncommon to see "For Sale" signs posted along Highway 101. It was as if the Japanese submarine I-25 had sunk Oregon Coast businesses too.

Able men and women were also drained from the coast. The men were enlisting in the armed forces, and the women went off to work in industrial plants where battleships and bombers were being built. While men fought the war abroad an aggressive advertising campaign attracted women into industrial plants as welders and riveters. A "Rosie the Riveter" phonograph record hit the top of the pop charts, and posters showing women doing a man's job in manufacturing plants made women feel they were fighting the enemy too. Then on May 29th 1943 Norman Rockwell's famous *Saturday Evening Post* depiction of "Rosie the Riveter" helped solidify America's war effort. Among those taking up that challenge was Joan S. Clayberger from Woodburn, Oregon, who wrote in *104 More Rosie the Riveter Stories*, "We worked on the ships from start to launching. During my senior year, I worked weekends and any days we had off from school. After graduation, I trained to be a burner and I did that until the war was over."

In Oregon and on the Coast people not already taken by the military and industrial plants volunteered for the Oregon Defense Council. Some worked on the roads. The Oregon Highway Commission was forced to hire women because of the shortage of men. In the Oregon Highway Commission's Sixteenth Biennial Report, the author writes that women were hired for "flagging of traffic, the driving of small trucks and other of the lighter tasks." In order to attract women the highway commission had to offer wages commensurate with other industries.

Even though tourism traffic slowed to a trickle, the Coast Guard did save some businesses from going under. They rented beach cabins for the patrolling forces and coast resorts for

Women at Work During World War II

Road
construction
flaggers

Drivers

Road crew

Oilers

Pavement steamroller drivers, 1940s

officer's headquarters. On the beach, Coast Guardsmen patrolled with 30-pound walkie-talkies, submachine guns, and dogs. At times it appeared the only people authorized to beachcomb were military personnel.

The Coast Guardsmen looked for saboteurs and invasions, reported shipwrecks and vessels in distress, watched for enemy planes, and confronted strange people. They also confiscated cameras, kept people off the beaches at night, enforced blackouts, and directed them away from fortifications, lookouts, and radar stations. By August of 1943 the war was going so well that the number of beach patrols was cut in half. The I-25 submarine that had caused such a fright was sunk in the central Pacific on September 3, 1943.

In August the first blimp hangar was complete. Twelve days later the second hangar was completed. These huge hangars were the largest wooden structures in the world. At least 1700 workmen had participated in building them.

Blimp hangar under construction. *Photo from the Tillamook Museum*

Coos Head Coast Guard Station

Cape Mears Lighthouse. *Photo by the Charles I. Clough Co.*

83

Original lighthouse at Newport, Oregon

Hangar "A" was 1072 feet long, 297.5 feet wide and 170 feet high. It dwarfed all the other buildings on the NAST (Naval Air Station Tillamook), including enlisted men's barracks, mess halls, officer's clubs, and nearby barns. The two hangars were so large that on August 21, 1950, Swede Ralston flew through

Taking the blimp out of the hangar; Naval Air Station in Tillamook

Eight blimps inside one hangar; Naval Air Station in Tillamook

Aerial view of Naval Air Station in Tillamook

A plane flying through the blimp hangar;

Hangar "B" in a North American AT-6 Texan Trainer, at 250 mph. The hangars were built with 51 wood-arched trusses. The engineers had used wood because steel was needed for the war effort. The trusses had to be uniquely designed for the domed roof. Each hangar housed eight K-type blimps that were 252 feet long, 79 feet high and 62 feet wide.

These blimps did reconnaissance, provided escort to ship convoys, carried out search and rescue operations, watched for Japanese mines in the Pacific, and kept watch for Japanese balloon bombs. Probably their most noteworthy service was as a submarine deterrent. As long as the blimps were floating over-head the submarine stayed under the water, slowing them to 4 knots. Of the numerous convoys that the blimps chaperoned, not a single ship was lost.

The blimp hangars provided the town of Tillamook with landmarks of incomparable size that would be noticed by travel-ers on Highway 101 for decades to come.

When it became apparent we were winning the war in Octo-ber of 1943, the Oregon State Defense Council was eased out of service. Then in 1944 "Dim Out" signs were removed from

Tillamook Cheese Company

Highway 101, and tourist travel began to return to the coast. Between 1941-1946 the Highway Commission limited their road work to essential roads supporting the war. They estimated it had cost $10,859,000, of which the federal government had paid $9,031,000, and the remainder was paid by Oregon. Some of the money went to projects along Highway 101. One of the costs was maintenance of existing roads because of heavy truck traffic, especially logging trucks. At that time the typical truck-load of Douglas fir taken from virgin forests was three logs. The logs were so long and heavy that road curves and intersections had to be appropriately compacted to withstand the extra weight.

Anticipating the war's end the Oregon State Highway Department began making plans for putting the returning servicemen to work on new highway projects all over Oregon. Major realignments were scheduled on Highway 101.

Then on May 8, 1945 "Victory in Europe" was proclaimed. In September of 1945 Japan surrendered. The war was over. Life along Highway 101 began to rev back up.

As early as 1917 politicians had been saying Oregon needed a military highway along its coast. Between 1941 and 1946, Oregon finally had one.

Post-War

Imagine a graph with lines representing tourism, economics, and road building on Oregon's coast. Before the war all of those lines would have been slanting upward. With the bombing of Pearl Harbor those lines dove off the chart like a kamikaze pilot on a suicide mission. On the Oregon Coast it was like the Depression all over again. When the war-ended gears shifted

Tillamook Pleasantville, 1949

Highway 101 between Winchester Bay and Clear Lake

Haystack Rock-Cannon Beach

Haystack Rock

forward. Thousands of men found work, building highways. Relics of the curvy Roosevelt Highway impeded traffic. The Oregon Coast Association pushed for funding and lobbied the state legislature to straighten and level the route.

Thousands of tourists from across the nation vacationed in Oregon each year between 1946 and 1950. A division of the Oregon State Highway Commission, the "Travel Information Department," was largely responsible for this uptick. They advertised Oregon in leading national magazines, 50 major newspapers, and films promoting the beauty of Oregon. Many of their promotional photographs were taken on Oregon's rugged coast. It was predicted that the tourist industry would bring in millions of dollars. In a meeting at Gearhart, of the Oregon Coast association in October, 1946, Governor Earl Snell pointed out that tourism was the third largest industry in the state generating nearly $100 million a year.

At another Oregon Coast Association meeting in October of 1947, Charles F. Walker, president of Northwestern School of Commerce, Portland, pushed the group towards a 6-point program to attract tourists: "1) Promote legislation to rid the highway of slow drivers, 2) improve the character of businesses on the coast, 3) improve telephone communications to the coast, 4) expand the association's membership, 5) reward outstanding businesses and, 6) improve the stature of celebrations on the coast." When he sat down, Charles F. Robinson president of the Association, concluded the meeting stating that 1947 was "the best tourist year the Oregon coast ever had."

Highway 101 near Heceta

Heceta Lighthouse

The jump in tourism increased business profits and new construction. In May of 1946, The Oregonian quoted Ira Clinton, a Yachats motel owner, "Even this early I'm full every night and turning people away. By June or August I'll have to make reservations a month ahead." Such statements were common, along with "No Vacancy" signs. Cash registers jingled in restaurants, grocery stores and gas stations. One newspaper headline blazed, "Major Real Estate Boom Enlivens Oregon Coast." There were new housing subdivisions, new motels, new resorts, new apartments, and all types of supporting businesses. Many new lumber mills opened too and lumber trucks thundered through cities.

Amateur photographers jockeyed to get shots of the trucks rumbling across coast bridges. Tourist advocates claimed the big trucks impeded traffic on the steep grades and curvy roads. Still, Oregon was outstripping every other state in its production of lumber. Even Washington dropped to second place. But it was the lure of nature and Oregon's majestic forests, amazing ocean

10-foot Sitka Spruce log, Bester & Vaughn Logging Co., Yachats, Oregon

Logging truck on Highway 101 near Cannon Beach

Highway 101 near Winchester Bay

Reedsport

sunsets, hunting, and fishing, which attracted tourists, sports-men, and renowned personalities. Western author Zane Grey settled up the Rogue River, and famed composer Ernst Bloch took up residency in Agate Beach, near Newport.

Just when all this activity was cresting, a sobering reminder of the war years shook Oregon. In November of 1947 on the Oregon Coast highway near Heceta Head a huge cloud of smoke drifted over the highway from a detonated Japanese mine. During the month of November, 20 mines were discovered off Oregon's coast, and the U.S. Coast Guard detonated most of them. A newspaper photograph shows a young man about five feet tall who discovered one on the beach at Gearhart. In the picture the 350-pound sphere looks enormous next to the young man. When the teen had cleared the scene, Navy experts deto-nated the mine.

While the beaches were being cleared of mines the Oregon Coast Association and the Oregon State Highway Commission went to work trying to make Oregon's highways safe and invit-ing. The Highway Commission suggested that Highway 101 be widened through the city of Gold Beach. On April 16, 1947 the city council approved the new plan. More Highway Commission projects were planned. The Highway Association was concerned about all the curves in the highway and demanded that they be straightened— especially on the south coast between Brookings and Gold Beach, where the highway detoured inland over hills to Carpenterville.

The highway department's engineer, R. H. Baldock, asked the state legislature to fund the straightening of the coast high-way. In 1949, they increased the gas tax and registration fee for automobiles to raise funding. Combined with federal alloca-tions, the funding was now available for the highway department to concentrate on its projects along Oregon's coast. They wanted to reduce the hazards of curves, reduce the number of steep grades, and include whenever possible turnouts for viewing the coast's scenic splendor.

Highway 101 as it looked in 1950 in Northern Coast Towns

Hot Plant

Cannon Beach

Rockaway

Garibaldi

Nehalem

Tillamook Bay City

One example of the highway commission's work was north of Cannon Beach. In 1950 a curvy, steep road four miles in length was straightened and a notorious uphill grade lessened. The road was relocated east, and when finalized had easy curves and just a 6 percent grade. Other examples of road alignments included roads north of Tillamook, north of Newport, and south of Reedsport. Through 1954 the highway department also upgraded highway surfaces to asphaltic concrete, added additional lanes for passing slow traffic on uphill grades, and in some instances increased two-lane roads to four. They also rebuilt wooden bridges and shored up slide-prone hillsides.

Delake Bridge collapsed in storm of January, 1939

Tourists from out of state benefitted from the improved and safer roads. Nearly 2,000,000 cars visited Oregon during 1953-54. The travel department had experimented with television advertising for the first time. In a popular highway magazine, Richard L. Neuberger, Oregon Senator wrote, "Like a lariat, U.S. 101 clings to the great headlands which the Oregon Coast Range thrusts down to the sea. With white-capped talons and plumes of spray, the tossing Pacific often seeks to unravel this asphalt

Yaquina Head Lighthouse, Newport

Umpqua Lighthouse

Tillamook Lighthouse

Near Tillamook Head

South Cannon Beach

Sunset Bay near Coos Bay

Sunset Bay

Jockey Cape, Northern Oregon coast

Highway 101 over Fogerty Creek north of Depoe Bay

noose. Few other roads on the continent thread a more spectacu-lar tightrope between mountains and salt water." Photographs by the famed photographer Ray Atkeson accompanied the article.

Of course Oregon's coast was not all pleasant and wonderful. During late summer in August and September there was the continual threat of forest fires—the famous Tillamook Burn of 1933 still hung in people's memories. Some loggers swore there was a six-year jinx because fires followed in 1939, 1945, and even in April 1951, when a large swath of forestland was wiped out east of Tillamook at Elkhorn Creek. In 1956 fires swept over tinder-dry forests east of Gardiner and hot weather conditions shut down lumber operations throughout western Oregon. In addition to the risk of fires there was also the continual threat of road slides brought on by rainy weather during the winter

Miner Creek Slide, Milepost 145

Spencer Creek Slide

1953 slide at Milepost 332

months. One slide in 1954 buried Highway 101 under fifty feet of dirt on Oregon's northern coast south of Nehalem.

Despite setbacks the Highway Commission plunged ahead with its many new projects. One editor wrote in 1956 that he was deeply concerned with the bottleneck in southern Oregon. The notorious stretch of highway between Brookings and Gold Beach was turning tourists away, he proclaimed. The road was narrow and had too many curves and steep grades. Logging trucks made it even more dangerous and slow. The twisty road hadn't changed much since the 1920s, when it was part of the Roosevelt Highway.

Another piece of the Roosevelt Highway, no longer accessible by car, lies up the hill from Humbug Mountain State Park. If you hike up the hill behind the campground, above the present day road, you'll find a remnant of the old highway that looks as it had been hit by a major earthquake. Parts of road bed are covered with dirt from slides, the rest is covered with moss, drying leaves and decaying trees.

Humbug Mountain; mouth of Brush Creek

The original highway at Humbug Mountain was very steep with tortuous curves. It was a notoriously bad part of the road. A staff writer for the *Oregonian* wrote, "The peak rears itself abruptly out of the waves and as the motorist winds up the long climb, sheep feeding on the steep hillside seem to be clinging there by use of magnetic feet." In 1955 the highway department put in new bridges and realigned the highway, removing the treacherous curves and reducing the steep grade. The new highway was sited along the meanders of Brush Creek. The route is safer and allows travelers to see ocean views.

About the same time and further north another section of the highway was being straightened and elevated—south from the outskirts of Depoe Bay a new 4.6-mile route over Cape Foulweather replaced the old Roosevelt Highway that twisted through the coastal community of Otter Crest. Relocating the road required huge earthmovers, tractors, scrapers, rollers, drills, portable compressors, backhoes, and loaders. The construction crews had to deal with water- saturated earth, boulders, heavy

New Highway 101
along Brush Creek

Depoe Bay

Otter Crest Park. *Drawing by F.G. Hutchinson, December 15, 1944*

timber, and steep hillsides. Yet, the new road uncorked another tedious and curvy bottleneck.

The old Otter Crest road was abandoned, blockaded with boulder and sturdy barricades. A year later, in 1956, residents and tourists complained they wanted to drive the slower picturesque Roosevelt Highway. Their complaints reached Governor Elmo Smith and it wasn't long before the boulders and fencing

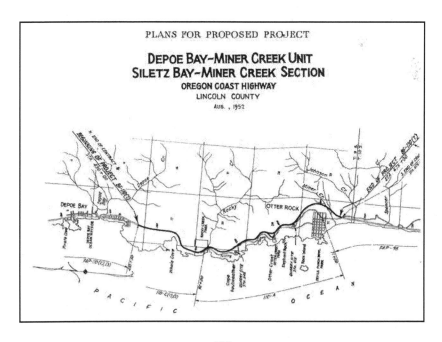

South from Otter Crest, Highway 101, ca 1940

were removed. Today, known as Otter Crest Loop, the traveler can turn off the Coast Highway and drive over a rehabilitated Rocky Creek Bridge. There they find a memorial to Benjamin Jones, often referred to as the father of the Roosevelt Highway. The historic old Highway continues south below Cape Foulweather, many popular roadside resorts, and Devil's Punch Bowl State Park. At the south end of the Otter Crest loop it rejoins the Coast Highway.

Another picturesque piece of the Roosevelt Highway was built in the 1920s and is still available for travel, crossing the Cascade Head Experimental Forest north of Lincoln City. Cascade Head is a scenic national research area of 11,890 acres established in 1934 to study typical coastal Sitka spruce-western hemlock forests. The acreage includes Cascade Head, a promontory that juts out into the Pacific Ocean beside the Salmon River estuary. The old Roosevelt Highway remains as a back road east of Highway 101, through the east half of the experimental forest south of Neskowin. The old highway curves through a mix of newer and old growth forests. If the traveler is interested in experiencing a 1920s forest road there is no better place on the

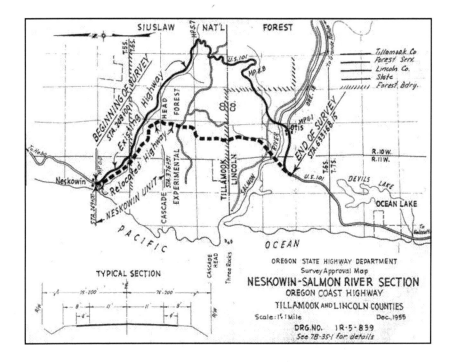

Oregon Coast to imagine where Model Ts once drove, and where you can ponder about another era while passing under trees that were standing before the road was built.

In 1957-59 the Bureau of Public Roads replaced the old road with a new section of Highway 101 between Neskowin and Otis Junction. The new, straightened road reduced the mileage from eleven miles to about six.

Meanwhile the Oregon State Highway Commission was working on another shortcut, between Coos Bay and Bandon. During the devastating fire of 1936, residents of Bandon fled on the Roosevelt Coast Highway to Coquille. From there the highway arced north and west for 18 miles before reaching Coos Bay.

The new highway alignment proposed by the highway commission would bypass Coquille, reducing the distance between Bandon and Coos Bay from 36 miles to about 23 and reducing the number of curves from 168 to 31. The highway

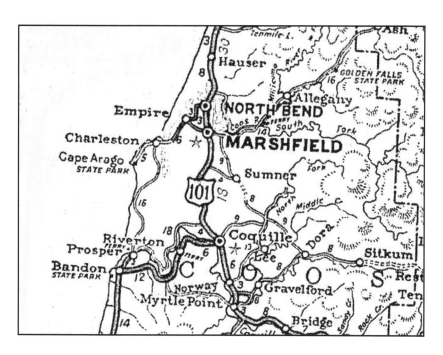

department undertook the building project with three separate road contracts. Between 1956 and 1960. The new road extended from Davis Slough, 7 miles south of Coos Bay, to the Coquille River, where it connected with the existing road that crossed Bullard's Bridge and led into the northern edge of Bandon.

Before the completed highway there was another westerly route from Bandon to Coos Bay. It was much longer and began at the historic Bullard's ferry crossing on the northern outskirts of Bandon. This old route meandered west and north through timberlands to Charleston on the Seven Devils Road. As traffic increased the slow-moving winch-operated ferry system became obsolete. According to Ray Allen's book, *Oregon Coast Bridges*, "In 1952, Coos County and the Oregon State Highway Department agreed to construct a new bridge across the Coquille River... known locally as Bullard's Bridge. It is one of only two steel vertical lift spans along the Oregon Coast." It is a magnificent bridge, designed with the guidance of Oregon's bridge engineer, Glen Paxson. The bridge was completed in 1954. Six years later the bridge would become part of the Highway 101

Bandon Beach

relocation project between Bandon and Coos Bay. The Roosevelt Highway from Bandon via Coquille to Coos Bay still exists today, and is now called Highway 42. Now, the turn off to Seven Devils Road is from Highway 101 north of Bullard's Bridge.

By the 1960s much of the old Oregon Coast Highway had been rebuilt, relocated, straightened and improved. Some of these sections included the highway from Bay City to Tillamook, Reedsport to Coos Bay, Port Orford to Gold Beach, and Brookings to the California state line. In 1957 two bottlenecks frustrated the Oregon Coast Association. The first was the famous curvy road from Brookings north to Gold Beach. It is possible to get an idea of how treacherous the road originally was in my novel, by reading, *Kidnapped On Oregon's Coast Highway* (1926). The road was muddy in winter, steep, and hardly fit for an automobile. In 1957 even though the road was paved it was still a corkscrew with steep grades. The road was so bad that many tourists traveling north from the Redwoods of California got discouraged and turned back. Members of the Coast Association lobbied to have the curves removed. If the Oregon State Highway Commission could remove them it would "uncork a golden flood of tourists from California," they said.

Old Roosevelt
Highway between
Brookings and Gold
Beach

Brookings to
California on
Highway 101

Highway 101
near Gardiner

Highway 101 between Reedsport and Winchester Bay

The Coast Association was hoping to persuade the Oregon State Legislature in February of 1957 to appropriate funds to build a new road from Brookings to Gold Beach. They also hoped $250,000 could be raised to assess the possibility of building a bridge over the Columbia River, from Astoria to Megler, Washington.

Myrtle trees along the Southern Oregon Coast Highway

Leveling Mountains

In the late 1950s and early 1960s the Oregon State Highway Commission planned one of its greatest construction projects ever, connecting Brookings and Gold Beach with a new relocated road west of the old road and through unbelievably rough terrain. When the road was completed it would plow through mountains, ford incredible gorges, make accessible pristine beach areas, and include one of Oregon's highest bridges—Thomas Creek Bridge. Completing this relocation of the Oregon Coast Highway would take almost five years.

The old road from Brookings to Gold Beach went inland from Brookings through Carpenterville. Then it dropped westward at Pistol River, where the road leveled out, going along the shoreline into Gold Beach. Originally the road was a trail. It was first leveled with mules tugging fresno-plows. The old road could only be travelled in the summer months, because of rocky outcrops, muddy bogs, and huge tree roots. The first automobile drivers took along winches, shovels, and picks for road emergencies. In the mid 1920s the highway commission, for lack of funds, put construction of the road on hold. It was probably the worst road in Oregon. It seemed southern Curry County had to wait for its road improvements until most of the remaining Coast Highway was built. Finally in the late 1920s the road was graded and rocked. In the 1930s it was paved. The Coast Association kept prodding the highway department to straighten the road. After all it was the southern entrance into Oregon.

The highway department ordered a reconnaissance survey in 1938, but the war intervened and the plan was shelved. After the war, the Coast Association broached the bottleneck problem again. They spurred the highway department to stop ignoring Curry County. The highway commission called for a new survey in 1951. The final survey line was run in 1957.

Even before the 1951 reconnaissance survey, Samuel H. Boardman had been trying to acquire enough property for a state park on the southern Oregon coastline. It would be his biggest triumph. Boardman is referred to as the father of the Oregon State Parks system. From its origination in 1929 to 1950 Boardman amassed over 66,000 acres of parkland for the state of Oregon. He retired in 1950 but most of the rugged Curry County parkland was acquired prior to his retirement. He was the first to recognize its value for preservation. He acquired 12 miles of parkland that majestically traversed Oregon's coast. Today the park is referred to as Samuel H. Boardman State Scenic Corridor. It has become one of Oregon's most picturesque parks, comprising 1471 acres. Samuel Boardman died in 1953 so he was not able to see how the new Highway 101 would access his work. The final highway survey line in 1957 sliced through Boardman Park for 10 miles.

It was spectacular terrain inhabited by deer, elk, bear, and cougars. The sixteen-mile proposed highway between Pistol River and Brookings included one 340-foot deep gorge that was

Cape Sebastian off scenic Highway 101 south of Gold Beach

Coastline near Brookings

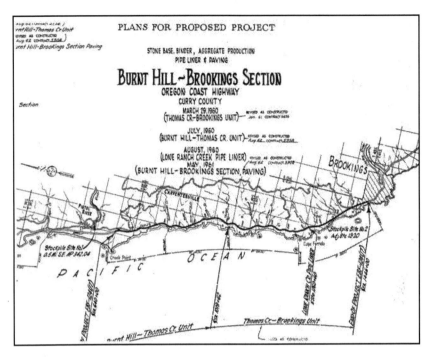

PLANS FOR PROPOSED PROJECT

STONE BASE, BINDER, AGGREGATE PRODUCTION
PIPE LINER & PAVING

BURNT HILL~BROOKINGS SECTION
OREGON COAST HIGHWAY
CURRY COUNTY
MARCH 29, 1960
(THOMAS CR~BROOKINGS UNIT)

JULY, 1960
(BURNT HILL~THOMAS CR. UNIT)

AUGUST, 1960
(LONE RANCH CREEK PIPE LINER)
MAY, 1961
(BURNT HILL~BROOKINGS SECTION, PAVING)

800-feet across—Thomas Creek Canyon. When completed the new relocated highway from Gold Beach to Brookings would be 27.7 miles, reducing the distance between the two towns by 8.5 miles and saving 25 minutes of driving time. The most difficult segment of this new road was the sixteen-mile stretch between Pistol River and Brookings. It was divided into four sections.

The huge project gained funding in 1957 when the Oregon State legislature appropriated $12,600,000 in the sale of bonds to fund the project. In 1958 the long awaited construction began. Some right-of-way difficulties had held back progress, along with a construction workers strike. When the dust settled the awarding of construction contracts began.

The first was awarded to Peter Kiewit and Sons' firm of Medford in January. The bid for $1,056,025 covered the section between Brookings and Cape Ferrelo, a distance of about 4 miles. They began by removing brush and trees and building a culvert for Harris Creek. The second contract was awarded in March to the Darkenwald-Harms Company of Sacramento,

Whalehead headland during Highway 101 construction between Pistol River and Brookings

Huge drainage pipes directing creeks to the sea

Aerial view of Highway 101 during construction at Whalehead

California, for the four-mile project between Cape Ferrelo and Thomas Creek. The bid called for grading and excavation work. Nearly half of the proposed relocated highway was under construction. In May the State Highway Commission awarded a third contract to the low bidder Peter Kiewit and Sons, for the 3.55 miles at the northern end of the project known as Burnt Hill to Hooskanaden Creek. This section required considerable excavation, preventative work to ward off landslides, and several large drainage structures.

As the weather improved so did the movement of big machinery through Brookings. In fact it may have looked like a New Year's Day Parade in New York, Big scrapers, bulldozers,

Brookings

Elk River Bridge

Massive 92-inch
drainage pipe
diverting water to
sea

Road-building machine

large Caterpillars, and other heavy equipment came rumbling through the town to aid men already clearing brush and removing trees. During construction more than $5 million of heavy equipment would be used. Over 85 men worked for the two companies. All this wasn't without an accident, two men died during the road building. One man was injured when he drove a big tractor on a weakened road and was unable to stop it from tumbling down a steep embankment. The man jumped off and only suffered a fractured leg.

The last part of the sixteen-mile stretch to be let out was the Hooskanaden Creek to Thomas Creek project. It was only three and a half miles but it was the highway department's most difficult section. It was granted to Morris-Knudsen Company for a bid of $2.5 million in July of 1958. *The Brookings Harbor Pilot* newspaper quoted a state official as saying the job was the "biggest single job ever let in the state." Not only was grading a part of the job but the company would have to move 4,115,000 cubic yards of earth.

Oregon State Highway Engineer W. C. Williams wrote, "In the 16 mile strip now being straightened, a record 11 million cubic yards of earth and rock must be moved." At Whalehead Creek, for example, the fill was nearly 250 feet high. The fill was excavated from nearby cuts. An *Oregonian* staff writer wrote, "Engineers consider the new road being constructed between Gold Beach and Brookings one of the wonder highways of the world. It is a distance of 34 miles and costing $18 million the most expensive piece of work ever undertaken by the state highway commission."

After the rugged terrain had been ripped apart by the heavy highway building machines, the coast terrain appeared to have been struck by hurricanes, earthquakes and tsunamis, especially between Hooskanaden Creek and Thomas Creek. Huge 96-inch drainage pipes, enough to stretch eight miles, were buried under hundreds of feet of earth in canyons to divert water from creeks to the sea. Mountains were torn off and used to fill the valleys,

Highway construction abutting on scenic Pacific Ocean

all the while trying to build a level roadbed with long straight-aways and easy sweeping curves. For this project it seemed as if there were two heavy construction machines, one moving north-ward from Brookings, grading, excavating, shoring up canyon walls, redirecting streams, and leveling ground. The other behemoth rumbled south from Pistol River, filling canyons and leveling mountains. When the two giants neared each other they each faced a formidable gulf—the 350-foot gorge at Thomas Creek.

Tallest Bridge

Jutting out from the south side of a gorge supported by two towering falsework pedestals was a large 30-foot-by-30-foot steel deck truss cantilevered 350 feet above the gorge creekbed. Dangling from the deck's tip were nets designed to catch workers should they slip and fall. Local high school students wanting a thrill would jump from the surface of the span into the dangling nets. Soon a watchman was hired to prevent accidents to teenagers and others.

This bridge would connect the newly constructed roads as the final link—the crown jewel.

Thomas Creek Bridge in upper left of photograph

At first engineers thought the construction of a steel-arched bridge would be the best choice for the gorge, following the theme of coastal arched bridges. But on inspection of the south slope it was determined unsuitable for an arched bridge foundation. Other designs were considered too, but the gorge site had many drawbacks; one was high wind, which limited the choice. Then it was decided to go with a steel-towered bridge designed by Ivan D. Merchant. This bridge would actually pass above the unstable south slope. The new bridge was somewhat like the Samuel Reed Bridge on Neahkahnie Mountain.

The Reed Bridge had six steel towers, was 602 feet long, and stood 85 feet above the creek bed. The Thomas Creek Bridge had two towers, was 848 feet long and stood 350 feet above the creek bed. It is Oregon's highest bridge and is higher then the Golden Gate Bridge, which averages 220 feet. Rising from the creek bed the two towers for the Thomas Creek Bridge appear almost too fragile to support 1700 tons of structural steel but they have endured heavy traffic and winter storms for decades.

Scenic view on Route 101 near Cape Sebastian. *Courtesy of the Oregon State Highway Commission*

Newly completed Thomas Creek Bridge with traffic

On April 12, 1960 the Oregon State Highway Commission awarded Bethlehem Steel Company of San Francisco (a subsidiary of Bethlehem Steel of Pennsylvania) the job of building the bridge. It entailed building a two-lane continuous deck-truss 30 feet by 30 feet, supported by two steel towers over the gorge. Construction began on the south slope and extended north on falsework pedestals. Cantilevered past each pedestal, the next pedestal was built, from the top down, with steel beams craned down from the bridge surface. The two main supporting towers were built as construction proceeded across the canyon. They rested on concrete piers 20 feet above the ground and forty feet below grade level. As the first tower was complete the falsework towers south of it were taken down. The whole process was one of precision teamwork and careful calculations.

The bridge and highway had garnered so much attention that Oregon's Governor Mark Hatfield was asked to attend the ceremony and dedicate them at their grand opening. The ceremony was scheduled for December 9, 1961. The Oregon Coast Association had organized the big event. Surprisingly, newspaper accounts of the dedication ceremony included few words about Oregon State Highway engineer W. C. (Dutch) Williams.

Williams had led the highway department for the previous five years, since 1956. A public relations release noted, "It was under Williams that the Interstate System of Oregon began." He supervised the building of 1, 585 miles of highway. He had spent his entire adult life working for the highway department. Starting as a transit man, he had slowly moved up through the ranks, working at most positions in the department. When H. R. Baldock resigned in 1956, Williams was appointed to replace him. Williams pledged to continue the "engineering competence" and the "intellectual and moral integrity" of his predecessor.

Of the route between Pistol River and Brookings, Williams wrote, "The work therefore represents some of the heaviest grading work ever undertaken in Oregon." He estimated the new highway would cost $11 million or about $730,000 per mile. Williams asserted, "The opening of this new section of highway will culminate almost 20 years of efforts by foresighted highway engineers who years ago recognized the eventual need for improving this section to modern standards and for opening to public view one of the most spectacular portions of the Oregon coastline."

Williams recognized that the Pistol River to Brookings highway relocation was Oregon's most massive project. He went about supervising its completion with considerable care. He was especially proud of slide prevention techniques that used a "tremendous amount of drainage pipe" which he felt made a difference. In addition the new highways elevation was only 465 feet above sea level where the old highway was 1715 feet at

Carpenterville. Also the maximum curvature of the new highway was only six degrees as compared to 56 degrees on the old road. It was a spectacular highway and he would have been proud had he been able to attend the dedication ceremony. But ten days before the dedication he died. On November 30, 1961 he passed away at the age of 65. Hatfield said of Williams, "Dutch Williams gave virtually his entire life to public service. The highway program of Oregon bears lasting witness to his engineering skill and administrative capacity." One engineering magazine claimed the completion of the Brookings to Gold Beach highway was a monument to Williams' work.

At the road opening ceremony on December 9th, 1961 in front of 1000 or more people, Governor Mark Hatfield used a baseball bat to smash the neck off of a bottle that symbolized the removal of another major Oregon bottleneck.

Typical rest areas along Oregon's coast included spectacular ocean vistas

Epic Achievement

The completion of the Oregon Coast Highway, some proclaimed, happened in 1932 with the building of the I. A.
Patterson Bridge across the Rogue River. The highway, at that
time, stretched south from the Columbia River to the California-
Oregon border, about 400 miles. Yet portions of the road still
needed paving, rocking, and oiling, and major rivers needed to
be bridged. The concept of the highway fit snugly in people's
imaginations, yet when they experienced the reality of the road
many questions came up.

Detours existed around construction sites, long lines frustrated the traveler at ferries, parents and children got carsick on
the many curves and automobiles' radiators blew up on steep
mountain grades. To complicate matters there was the road
designation itself. Was it the Oregon Coast Highway or Highway
101, the federal designation for interstate highways? The highway had many contradictions.

In 1936 five major bridges were built over the coastal rivers
and bays, making aficionados say the highway was now complete. But was it safe with existing bottlenecks? Then in the post-
war era the highways were straightened and leveled and major
bottlenecks were removed. By 1963 most Oregonians might
have thought, "Now our coast highway is finished!"

But one mighty gap still remained—the Columbia River.
What visionaries had imagined in 1917 was a military highway

from Canada to the Mexican border. The federal government had sought to create it on paper when in 1924 they unveiled the idea of Highway 101, a north-south interstate highway. Although Highway 101 was listed on national and Oregon State maps, it was not a finished thoroughfare. The Oregon Highway Association pushed for more improvements and the completion of Highway 101 from Canada to the Mexican border. At last this dream seemed reachable—if only Oregon and Washington could agree on the complicated issues surrounding the financing and building of a bridge across the Columbia River.

Over 2000 ships have been lost on the treacherous bar of the Columbia River. It is known as the "Graveyard of the Pacific." One very obvious testament to the difficulty of entering the Columbia's tricky bar is the skeletal remains of the popular tourist attraction the *Peter Iredale*. It didn't even make it to the mouth of the river but sank about four miles south of the bar in 1906, snagged by the sand at Clatsop Spit. Had the *Peter Iredale* made it to the tricky Columbia bar it would have needed the expert help of the Astoria pilots. Beginning in the mid 1800s they captained incoming ships across the tricky bar, through the deep channels and away from the many shoals that threatened to capture commercial steamers. The service of having an Astorian

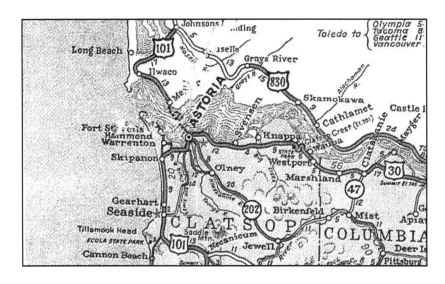

Wreck of the *Peter Iredale,* Clatsop County

captain pilot a ship through the channel was started with Captain George Flavel back in 1852.

Ten miles east of the bar, on the south side of the Columbia River, is the town of Astoria. Although the city is inland, its access is threatened by the river's turbulence and shifting sand shoals, like famous *Desdemona,* named after the American ship lost in 1857. The waters calm somewhat during the summer months. In the summer of 1840 one enterprising man, a poorly paid schoolteacher, lashed two canoes together and started a passenger and freight business across the precarious river. Joseph Leahy wrote, "All types of boats....made use of the river for ferrying people and goods between Oregon and Washington." By the early 1900s the freight business needed to include automobiles. A road from Portland to Astoria had been built along the banks of the Columbia River, and traffic south of Astoria began dribbling in due to the progress being made on the Roosevelt Highway. In 1921 one enterprising gentleman, Frits Elfving, known familiarly as the "Big Swede" or the "Crazy Swede" understood the need for a ferry system. Staking his small savings on the idea of a ferryboat, he commissioned the building of *Tourist I* to carry 14-15 cars across the river. The new ferry made its first trip from Astoria to McGowan, Washington on May 28, 1921.

Business prospered, so Captain Elfving had to order additional ferries; the *Tourist II* was built in 1924, and the *Tourist III* in 1931. In suitable weather Captain Elfving made 12 to 15 trips a day working practically every day. In 1946 the captain sold his business to the Oregon State Highway Commission for $163,000. The highway department ran the ferry until 1966, when the Astoria-Megler Bridge was finished.

In an article written for The *Sou'Wester* historical magazine, in 1991, former Washington State Senator Robert C. Bailey wrote, "It is said that Doc Steinman of the engineering firm of Robinson and Steinman, New York, picked the Astoria-Megler bridge site in 1928 or 1929." In 1930 the Longview Bridge was built, connecting Longview Washington to Rainier, Oregon. People in Astoria wanting to cross the river could either take the 45-minute drive to Rainer or wait in long lines to take the 35-minute unreliable ferry trip at Astoria. The ferry was subject to all sorts of delays due to bad weather, engine breakdowns, and the shifting Desdemona Sands. At that time there was no road paralleling the river on the Washington side.

In 1933 Washington's Pacific County, Oregon's Clatsop County, and the city of Astoria formed the "Oregon-Washington Bridge Trustees organization dedicated to building of a bridge across the river. In the Depression the building of roads and bridges was seen as a way to put men back to work. Plans for Oregon's central coast bridges were submitted to the Public Works Administration with the aid of the Oregon State Highway Department. But the bridge across the Columbia lacked that backing.

Nonetheless, the Bridge Trustee Organization forwarded their funding requests to the WPA. The bridge was projected to cost $5,500,000—to be financed with a loan for $3,850,000 to be paid off by a toll, and the remainder by a federal grant.

The Columbia River Bridge request was received on August 2, 1934 by the WPA and put "under examination." The United States Congress considered and passed a bill authorizing construction of the bridge; in the same year the WPA approved the Coos Bay and Yaquina Bay bridges. Later in 1935 the Astoria Bridge project was unequivocally rejected. Many reasons surfaced for the refusal. It was said that there would not be enough traffic to pay off the huge loan using the toll system. There was not enough economic or tourist activity on Washington's south coast. It was deemed a bridge to nowhere. Major business enterprises in the Willamette Valley exerted political pressure to defeat it. The Congressional bill supporting construction was for a limited time, yet every time the bill came close to expiring it was extended. In 1945 President Truman signed the Astoria Bridge Bill. Even with the President's approval, lingering hardships from the war and unsuccessful attempts at locating revenue sources kept the bridge idea from taking off. In 1946 the Oregon State Highway Commission became involved by purchasing the Astoria Ferry system from Captain Frits Elfving.

US 101 bottleneck at Columbia River ferry crossing

Old Fisher Hotel Astoria

Finnish
fisherman
drying and
preserving
their nets

Finnish, Swede
and Norwegian
princesses

Finnish fisherman and his daughter mending his nets

A typical ferry used to cross the Columbia River

The ferry system at Astoria started in 1921 and would remain active until 1966. For forty-five years the ferries became a way of life for the citizens of Astoria. From the kitchens of the hillside homes wives watched the landings and waited patiently on foggy days to see the ferries head out, stalwartly fighting currents as they crossed the river to Washington. Ticket takers, crewmen, and café operators all adjusted their lives to the ferry schedules. The ferry business was as much a part of Astoria as the sawyer was to the logging industry or the cannery worker to the canneries. Weather permitting there were 10 round trips in the winter between 6:30 A.M. and 8:00 P.M. and 20 in the summer with the last trip at 8:45 P.M.

Fishing boats

The Oregon State Highway Commission contracted the ferry business out to an independent business, Babbidge and Holt, but retained ownership of the three ferry boats and landings. The ownership forced the commission into new relationships. One was with Washington's Pacific County because the ferry service needed an adequate landing facility at Point Ellice. The others were the Port of Astoria and Washington's Toll Bridge Authority.

In the 1950s the Oregon State Highway Commission came face to face with a growing problem. More and more cars wanted to get to Washington via Astoria. Many arrived from the south up Oregon's Coast Highway only to wait in long lines at the ferry terminal. The ferries could not handle all the cars. The overload forced people up the river to the bridges at Longview or Vancouver. Many northbound tourists would turn off early and bypass Astoria altogether. Astoria was losing valuable tourist trade. The Oregon State Highway Commission was caught in the middle because on the one hand they promoted and advertised nationally the beauty of Oregon's coast, but on the other hand were criticized for inadequate ferry services. The commission was beginning to realize the importance of a bridge.

Finally a unifying force began sewing the different organizations and people together. In the early 1950s the Port of Astoria, directed by R. J. Bettendorf, led the battle for a bridge, along with Charles DeFoe manager of the Astoria Chamber of Commerce. A feasibility study was undertaken in 1953, funded by the Oregon State Highway Department, the Washington Toll Bridge Authority, Pacific County in Washington and the Port of Astoria. Each entity put up $12,500 for a total of $50,000. One important question was raised by the study: Traffic was not great enough for tolls to pay off revenue bonds in excess of 50 per cent of the total cost of the bridge. Other means of financing would have to be arranged. The federal government didn't have a program in place to help out.

By 1957 the bridge issue became a legislative matter. The legislatures of both Oregon and Washington appropriated

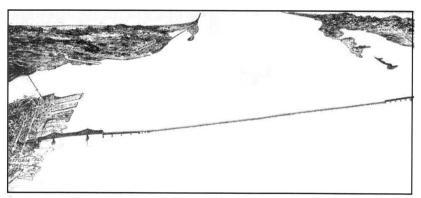

Proposed bridge looking west to mouth of Columbia River

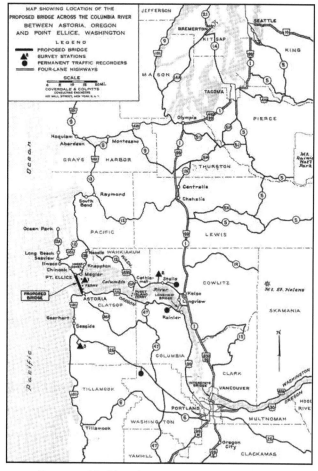

Proposed bridge from Astoria to Pt. Ellice

$100,000 to prepare final plans for the bridge. The Oregon State Highway Commission and the Washington Highway department began exhaustive studies.

On August 14, 1957 Bill McGrath interviewed Assistant State Highway Engineer Glenn Paxson for KAST radio in Astoria. Some of the questions and answers follow:

McGrath: Who will make the actual study?

Paxson: Under this agreement the State of Oregon will conduct the survey, study of the location and alignment and the determination of the most appropriate type of structure for the project.

McGrath: Tell me, Mr. Paxson, what types of design would generally be considered for making a crossing as long as this one?

Paxson: For this particular crossing the probable type would be a cantilever truss over the main ship channel near the Oregon shore. This truss would have to provide a vertical clearance of 198 feet because this part of the Columbia River is rated by the Navy as essential for national defense and would probably have to give a horizontal clearance of around 1,100 feet to satisfy the needs of navigation.

McGrath: I suppose the 198 feet would clear the largest type of ship?

Paxson: Yes it would.

McGrath: Now, how would the rest of the bridge be constructed?

Paxson: As soon as we get across the main channel, we then would drop down on as steep a grade as feasible and cross the Desdemona Sands an a viaduct which would be high enough to be safe from wave action. Near the Washington shore there is a secondary channel which is occasionally used by smaller ships. The crossing of this secondary channel may be on a grade high enough for a fixed structure or it may be more feasible to hold to a lower grade line and put in a drawbridge of some kind.

McGrath: Mr. Paxson, you mentioned a moment ago that the main span would most likely be a cantilever type, what well-known bridge in Oregon is of cantilever design?

Paxson: The McCullough Bridge over Coos Bay on Highway 101 is a cantilever bridge.

McGrath: What is the principal of a cantilever bridge?

Paxson: A cantilever bridge consists of three spans one on each end being an anchor span. From the anchor spans we continue out until we meet in the middle. The spans are connected so that the anchor spans help hold up the main span.

McGrath: What would be the approximate length of the bridge?

Paxson: The length of the structure would be approximately 4.1 miles. Of course the approaches would extend out considerably beyond that.

McGrath: Mr. Paxson, what special problems do you foresee in the design of this bridge?

Paxson: Because of the exposed location the wind forces which the bridge must withstand will be quite high, and with a two-lane bridge the width between trusses complicates provisions for taking care of these wind stresses.

Another problem concerns the viaduct portion of the bridge. A considerable portion of the length of the structure will be the viaduct across the Desdemona Sands where relatively short spans are feasible. Selection of the span for this portion must be carefully studied to hold the cost of the structure to a minimum.

At this point of growing public awareness many supported the bridge but some still claimed it was a bridge to nowhere.

They scoffed, asking who wanted to go from Astoria to Ilwaco? They said the bridge idea was a boondoggle of epic proportions, and there would not be enough money generated by the toll to pay off the $24 million needed to build the bridge.

State Senator Dan Thiel of Clatsop County said in a later interview with the *Eugene Register-Guard*, "They said no one would use our bridge....But I still remember ferry lines of people waiting. My daughter worked a summer at the landing just good-humoring people waiting with their kids in their cars."

Important political leaders began supporting the bridge. In 1957 William Holmstrom from Gearheart was elected state representative. He would claim later the eventual building of the bridge was his greatest satisfaction. In 1959 Mark Hatfield was elected governor of Oregon. He pledged the help of all the resources of his office to build the bridge. The governor, state senator Daniel Thiel, state representative William Holmstrom, Astoria's Bettendorf and Charles Defoe worked together to champion a bill that would pass through Oregon's state legislature.

Their bill also needed the consent of the Washington state legislature and governor. Before the final passage, political wrangling between the two states ensued. Joint meetings were held behind scenes to work out a compromise that could pass both legislatures.

In early April 1961 the Oregon State Senate, led by Dan Thiel, state senator from Clatsop County, voted on House Bill No. 1457 to build the Columbia River Bridge. During the meeting more than half of the senators slipped out of the room. When Senator Thiel called for a vote there were not enough present to constitute a quorum. One news report wrote that Thiel was terribly shaken. Suddenly those who had left the room began filtering back to their seats with big smiles on their faces. A new vote was taken and the Oregon State Senate voted 26-1 in favor of the bill. One senator later said "If we didn't like Dan Thiel, we wouldn't do this to him."

Co-sponsor of the House Bill 1457 was William Holmstrom. State representative Holmstrom led the battle for approval in Oregon's house—it passed 48-7. On April 27, 1961 Mark O. Hatfield signed the bill into law. The Washington legislature also passed its version of the bill, which was signed into law by Washington's Governor Albert Rosselini.

The bill signed into law by the two states essentially called for Oregon to float general obligation bonds amounting to $24 million and have charge of the engineering and construction of the bridge. Washington's Pacific County had to finance the north approach. If the toll was insufficient to pay off the loans and a deficit were to occur, Oregon was bound to pay the first $100,000 and any additional debt was to be paid on a 60-40 basis up to $200,000. At long last, after 30 years, there was a certain pathway to build a bridge.

In Astoria news of the bridge's approval shook the town silly. Parades honoring local leaders swept through town with a festive atmosphere. One of the jubilant participants may have stopped to look innocently across the four-mile expanse of the Columbia River and ponder, "How in the world will they build a bridge there?"

In September of 1961 the Oregon and Washington State highway departments entered into an agreement to build the bridge. The completed studies on the bridge from previous legislative acts had been submitted and approved by both Oregon and Washington legislatures. The detailed report included studies on location, navigation, designs, foundations, wind, materials, stream currents, and estimates of the final costs. On January 4, 1962, the Oregon State Highway Commission assigned resident bridge engineer Robert W. Ellison to the project. Active construction on the bridge began on November 5, 1962.

In a wildly delirious ceremony in Astoria, August 11, 1962 a thousand people crowded around Governor Hatfield and other prominent Oregon and Washington state dignitaries. Master of

Ceremonies Glenn Jackson, Oregon State Highway Commission chairman, introduced the Governor.

In his speech Governor Hatfield praised Senator Dan Thiel and Representative Bill Holmstrom, "because these are two men who have fought the hardest, I believe." To Washington's Governor Albert Rosellini's representative he gave a bronze plaque, "Hands Across the Columbia." The representative said, "In three years we can be back here again and we'll shake hands across the bridge."

The Governor then stated proudly that the five major coast bridges built in 1936 cost a total of five and a half million dollars, "and that all five of these bridges combined end to end would not be as long as this new bridge which we are starting today." He went on to say that in the 13-year period between 1951 through 1964 the state would spend over $85 million on Highway 101. "It can be truly said that Oregon is rolling ahead,

Governor Mark Hatfield digging the first shovel full of dirt

that progress is ours today....Thank you for this opportunity and we will proceed now to break ground."

Leaders at the event handed Hatfield a gold shovel. He then dug the first shovel full of dirt that represented, officially, the beginning construction of the Astoria-Megler Bridge.

Upper left of photo shows the beginning of steel structure over the main channel

Concrete pillars designed to support bridge approach from Astoria

"Spanning the Columbia River was a challenge in itself," said resident engineer Robert Ellison. One of the main problems was locating the piers. The Oregon Highway Department had to determine their exact locations before any work could start. Precise calculations were essential so that all the spans could be fitted in place. It took five months of detailed survey work before the engineers arrived at the final pier location measurements.

Five contracts were let for building the bridge: 1) The construction of 32 piers, 2) The building of 1,467 feet of the Oregon approach, 3) The steel superstructure, 4) Desdemona Sands Viaduct, and 5) the building of the Washington approach. The total length of the bridge was to be 21,697 feet. The Delong Corporation of New York was in charge of installing the 32 piers at a bid cost of $7,868,033. George Bauer, 52, foreman for the company, was the first and only fatality. He was killed when working on a specially designed river construction barge; a swinging broken cable knocked him into the river. Although extensive searches were made his body was never recovered. The accident led to Delong's inability to finish the job. According to Glenn Jackson:

Delong ran into difficulties very early in the program, having lost his foreman who was killed on the job. This foreman was apparently well qualified, as there was no trouble up to that point. Soon after the accident, difficulties began developing. When it became evident that Delong could not finish the job, the contract was cancelled and rebid on the original specifications.

The Oregon State Highway Commission sued Delong Corporation for damages. In the prolonged court battle the Highway Commission prevailed and in 1971 was awarded damages. The completion date that had originally been estimated for 1965 was now extended to 1966. Raymond International Inc. of New York City was awarded a new contract to complete the pier work on July 13, 1964. Work on the piers resumed in the summer of 1964 and continued into the spring of 1965.

New Young's Bay Bridge

Meanwhile the new Young's Bay Bridge was completed south of Astoria. The new crossing rerouted Highway 101 southwest from Astoria across Young's Bay to connect with the Coast Highway south of Warrenton. The straightened alignment of the new highway shaved miles off the old route. It also left an old portion of the Roosevelt Highway intact. For an excursion into the past, don't miss this drive.

Taking the old Roosevelt route south from Astoria is a scenic experience like none other in the United States. The old highway includes two historic bridges: the Old Young's Bay Bridge, a double-leaf bascule built in 1921 and the Lewis and Clark River Bridge, a steel single-bascule built in 1924. These bridges are historical examples of a bascule type of bridge. A bascule bridge is where the roadway tilts up out of the way of river traffic using counter weights as counterbalance. They are either single or double leaf. The old route loops inland to the south before turning west to connect back up with the new Coast Highway.

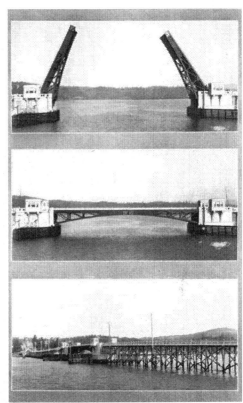

Old Young's Bay Bridge
on the Roosevelt Coast
Highway south of Astoria

Concrete approach to steel superstructure

Nearly completed steel superstructure over main channel

Workers pouring concrete

Last ferry trip

Back at the Columbia River workmen faced many obstacles in the completion of the bridge—high winds, rain, tides, daily ferries and incoming merchant ships. The Astoria pilots guiding commercial steamers had to be especially alert to river barges, cranes, cofferdams and boats coming to and from the river construction sites. From the contractor's point of view, the large incoming boats would sometimes come dangerously close to the river work due to the powerful tides. Barges with lights, reflectors and bells were set up. The men working on the water had to be given enough warning in order to get out of the way when collisions threatened.

By the end of 1965 the bridge's steel superstructure lacked only one key span— a 351-foot steel deck truss weighing 400 tons. Engineer Ellison had commented on this unique type of bridge building. "The spans were prefabricated on barges at Vancouver, Washington, and then transported by barge to the bridge site." This last section was floated to the bridge site and

Astoria toll station

connected with the rest of the bridge. Once in place workmen would lay decking in the winter months. Cheers resounded as the last section sailed into position on the north end of the superstructure in December of 1965.

The bridge opened on Friday, July 29th, 1966, about one month before the scheduled official dedication ceremony. The *M.R. Chessman* ferryboat made its last run across the river at 10:30 p.m. On the trip passengers were chaperoned by a full moon and the nostalgic awareness that this was the ending of an era. The next day at 6 a.m. the Astoria-Megler Bridge opened for one-way traffic. Pilot cars led the traffic through and around the finishing debris, painters, polishers, and rail builders.

If you had been driving to the new bridge from Astoria's Marine Drive that morning you would have first noticed the large concrete pillars that elevated the road leading to the super-structure. Your first stop at the base of the ramp would have been the toll station. After paying the toll of $1.50 cents you would have passed by the toll plaza building housing tourist information and other governmental offices. Then you would have waited in line for the pilot car to lead the cars across. The train of cars would have arced around on prestressed concrete beams climbing toward the next section of road. On the elevated road, above Marine Drive, you might have seen Astoria's historic hillside homes to the east and Astoria's businesses below. Still gaining altitude you would have driven on a steel decked truss section to the most scenic part of the bridge, the three-span through truss section that soared over the main Columbia River channel.

Engineer Ellison claimed it was the longest through truss in the world, stretching 2,464 feet. It consisted of three spans: 616 feet, 1232 feet, and 616 feet. The apex of the 1232 foot section, supported by concrete and steel towers, is 200 feet above the

West view showing completed bridge

river. Underneath there is room enough for the biggest military ships to pass. The horizontal width of the shipping channel is 1,070 feet. Through this channel huge commercial steamers guided by Astoria pilots would chug toward Portland.

If you had been driving over the bridge's high point on that July day in 1966 you would then have passed down over the very section of the steel superstructure that had been installed last—the steel-decked truss of 351 feet. After three more of these trusses the road then changes to 4 spans of steel plate girder sections, 150 feet long, leading to the famous viaduct that passes over the troublesome Desdemona Sands. Othello, fear not because Desdemona has been tamed! Dropping from 200 feet the roadway is now at 25 feet above mean sea level. Skimming over Desdemona, river views stretch east and west as you drive the next 11,200 feet on prestressed concrete spans. Approaching the northern bank, the viaduct section changes from concrete to steel plate girders. Here the northern part of the bridge, changes yet again with seven 351-foot-long steel through truss spans, crossing over the Washington shipping channel 49 feet below. A 150-foot steel girder span carries drivers down to the Megler approach.

Bridge Salute

While high-powered speedboats raced from Portland to Astoria on the Columbia River trying to be the first boat to whir under the new bridge, the sun lifted in the east, an extraordinary occurrence for this rain-drenched coastal city, and lit up a staging area where over 30,000 people were assembling. A parade with over 100 entries marched toward the tollbooth along Marine Drive. The ferryboat *M. R. Chessman* was gliding into the Astoria dock filled with passengers. Traffic was backing up at the bridge entrance. On this day the bridge crossing was free along with free rides on the ferryboat.

The Astoria High School band was assembling in front of the staging area with their music stands, costumes and instruments. Behind them dignitaries shook hands, smiled and climbed the bleachers. The local radio station was testing the microphones and radio feeds. Highway commissioners from both Washington and Oregon edged toward the platform. Oregon's governor Mark O. Hatfield and Washington's governor Daniel J. Evans, surrounded by staff, walked toward the rostrum. The dedication ceremony for the Columbia River Bridge was scheduled to begin at 2 p.m. It was Saturday August 27, 1966.

Originally the Oregon Coast Highway had been a curvy, slow route more than 400 miles long. But it had been a thread of life for people who lived along its path. Interminable years would pass before the highway could truly be called finished. Between 1924-5 when the designation Highway 101 was established, until the Astoria Megler Bridge dedication ceremony in 1966, Oregon's coast highway remained uncompleted. Highway 101 stretched 1,625 miles. In 1966 Oregon's share of that highway was about 344 miles, having been reduced by relocating roads that eliminated curves and steep mountain grades. It seemed at times that the people and leaders of Astoria were the only people in Oregon who recognized the need to build the final bridge. Now in 1966 Oregon's part of US Highway 101 would at long last be complete.

Written in the dedication program were these words: *"With the dedication of this magnificent structure, the Astoria Bridge, the last major obstacle in a continuous vehicular route along the pacific coast between Mexico on the south and Canada on the north has been eliminated."*

Reverend H. Robert Grossman delivered the invocation. Master of Ceremonies was Glenn L. Jackson chairman of the

Bridge superstructure over main channel

4.1-mile-long Columbia River Bridge

Oregon State Highway Commission. He rued the commission's decision to give the bridge a "secondary priority." Yet, once the commission recognized the need for a bridge they were the ones who pushed for its completion. He added, "With the shorter work weeks, with increases in pay and growth of leisure—our tourist boom has just begun." Jackson then introduced Elmer C. Huntley, chairman of the Washington State Highway Commission. "I believe this bridge will surpass its timetable. It is a magnificent structure."

After Huntley came Dan Evans Governor of Washington. The governor kept his speech short. He said, "we want this bridge to start paying for itself." He added "We will take the tolls off this one before schedule." Governor Mark O. Hatfield was introduced next. In a gracious gesture he gave the flag from the retired *M. R. Chessman* ferryboat to Mrs. Chessman, the widow of the great Astorian, Merle Chessman who had bravely written against the Ku Klux Klan. Before Merle Chessman passed away in 1947 he had argued for the need for more taxes for education, and for the building of the Oregon Coast Highway. Back in 1935 he had been one of the first to advocate building the Astoria Bridge.

Daniel J. Evans, Governor of Washington

Bridge opening ceremony

Two proud governors

North view from Astoria

Governor Hatfield, and Governor Evans then went with Miss Washington and Miss Oregon to the swinging gates blocking traffic to the bridge. The gates were tied together with ribbons, and two big bows. The ladies unraveled the bows and the governors pulled back the gates. The new Columbia River Bridge, the new Astoria-Megler Bridge, was officially open. A photograph commemorated the occasion with the two governors shaking hands in the foreground and the gleaming new bridge in the background.

The last bottleneck in the Oregon Coast Highway and Highway 101 was finally removed.

The Columbia River Bridge

About the Author:

E ven though he was born in California and earned a degree in history from San Diego State College, Joe Blakely has lived most of his life in Eugene, Oregon, where his various careers have included selling and appraising real estate, repairing and refinishing furniture, and working with the Office of Public Safety at the University of Oregon before his retirement in 1999. He resides in Eugene, with his wife Saundra Miles.

Joe Blakely with wife Saundra Miles on the Oregon Coast

His first book was *The Bellfountain Giant Killers*, the miraculous story of a little high school winning a state basketball championship in 1937. It received so much attention that Mr. Blakely felt he may have found a niche. His third book was *Lifting Oregon Out of The Mud: Building the Oregon Coast Highway.* This compelling historical story includes unbelievable construction photographs of the 1936 coast bridges. This book completed the first phase of building the Oregon Coast Highway. A subsequent novel *Kidnapped: On Oregon's Coast Highway-1926* has remained popular. His new book *Building the Oregon Coast Highway, 1936-1966* resumes the interesting struggle facing Oregonians as they built one of the most spectacular highways in the world.

For an autographed copy of Mr. Blakely's books, *Building Oregon's Coast Highway, 1936-1966* and *Lifting Oregon Out Of the Mud*, Please send a check for $17.95 plus $3.00 shipping to: Joe R. Blakely, PO Box 51561, Eugene, Oregon, 97405.

66702846R00096

Made in the USA
Columbia, SC
22 July 2019